# THE BLACK CARPENTER'S GUIDE

# THE BLACK CARPENTER'S GUIDE

How to succeed in construction
"From a black man's perspective"
WHAT YOU CAN DO TODAY
to put your career on the
fast track to success

Desmond Collins

**To order additional copies of this book, contact:**
Xlibris
1-888-795-4274
www.Xlibris.com
Orders@Xlibris.com
731388

# TABLE OF CONTENTS

Construction Terms:
Discover basic construction terms contractors and tradesmen use for effective communication in the construction field.

# FIRST EDITION

## The Black Carpenter's Guide

## To Construction

# WHAT YOU MUST KNOW NOW
to put your career on the
fast track to success

# DEDICATIONS

To all the tradesmen in the construction industry who paved the way for me and many other people of color, my sincere thanks

I would also like to dedicate this book to my loving wife Dawn Rae Collins. Without her continuing encouragement and help with spelling and vocabulary, this book would not have been possible.

I would also like to dedicate this book to my sons Marcus Desmond Collins and Malcolm Rashawn Collins who through their birth made me look at myself and grow into a man. Without the challenge of fatherhood and being a dad I may have not pushed myself as hard and looked at greater income and career opportunities, in which case this book may have not been accomplished.

"This book gives precise steps and teachings from training, heavy equipment, seeking employment and keeping employment in the competitive world of trade construction. In closing , I very much appreciated the deep insight on the personal struggles and strives being an African American black man in construction Desmond illustrates."

"Good read, educational and powerful!"

Curtis Oliver
Sheet metal/HVAC
Installer
Pacific Rim
Mechanical

"This book THE BLACK CARPENTER'S GUIDE TO CONSTRUCTION is an excellent resource to students, educators, and construction professionals. In reviewing this book, the principal criteria included content, organization, and reference sources. It clearly States history of early Black carpenters in constructions of Egyptian pyramids and temples to current contributions of Black carpenters in modern times and in California particular.

The book is organized into 16 easy to follow chapters, starting The right mind set as how to provide ones self to be successful in the industry. The later chapters guide readers the methods to obtain contracts, including trade associations to get leads.

Later subjects introduce reader the challenges, obstetrical, safety issues, tools of trades as well as relationship building and methods to be a successful carpenter.

This is maliciously explains step by step of carpentry work that only can be written by a master carpenter with long time on hands on experience. "

M M Zomorrodian
PE,RCE,GC , Associate Broker
cell 760-845-3146
CAL BRE # 01156545

# PREFACE TO THE FIRST EDITION

This guide is crucial reading for any black man or woman thinking about a career in construction. This guide will also be helpful for *any carpenter, labor or tradesman* who wants to excel in construction and has bigger aspirations than just digging trenches or cleaning up construction sites. The construction industry is dynamic and exciting and has plenty of opportunities to earn a good living. Unfortunately, the playing field is not always fair for people of color or minorities who would like to enter this field. I wish I could say that all you had to do is work as hard and as smart as the next man or woman and you would be given the same opportunities for advancement. That's just not the case. Having worked in the construction field for over 20 years, I am what you would call a first generation carpenter. What that means is that I had no family members in the field to help me land a job or give me any advice. Everything I learned about the trade is from the school of hard knocks. The purpose of this book is so you can learn from my mistakes. You will learn what works and what doesn't work. That way you will not be wasting valuable time and can focus on perfecting your skills as a journeyman carpenter. By reading this guide you have shown that you want more out of the field of construction than most people and will take the time and effort to learn the insider secrets to the field of construction. I congratulate you on your journey as you progress and advance in this field.

# ABOUT THIS BOOK

*This book was written with the black, African American, carpenter in mind. There are many books out there about construction but none that talk about the issues that confront the black carpenter.*

The subject matter in this book is laid out in a well thought out and progressive manner. Many hours of dedication and care have gone into its completion. It starts with developing the right mindset. From this foundation all the necessary character traits essential for success in the construction field are explained clearly in simple language. Next we explore the Black Contractors Association and the resources available for inner-city black men and women seeking training in the construction trades. Since its conception its goal has been the training of master builders and tradesmen from the labor pool of black communities. Learn about apprenticeship training and the differences between the apprenticeship programs. Staying healthy and avoiding injuries explains correct lifting techniques that prevent serious back injuries, as well as the different types of PPE, an acronym for personal protective equipment that is designed to protect you the worker from injuries.

Then we jump into the Union versus non-union companies, and go into detail about the benefits of belonging to the United Brotherhood of Carpenters or the AGC Associated General Contractors of America and will inform you on how to make an informed decision on which one will make more sense depending on your goals and career paths. You will also find out about the tools of the trade: what tools you should purchase, the bags you should wear and the clothing and PPE's that are required to work on construction sites. We explore details about cordless and specialty tools and the different brands that carpenters use out in the field. Discover the different building materials used in the construction field.

Learn about the different applications that fasteners can be used in on a building and what ones work best in special circumstances. Building systems reveals modern construction practices and systems carpenters and tradesmen use today out in the construction field to construct buildings and structures. Trade Specializations takes a look at all the different trades and specializations the construction field offers black workers. In applying at job-sites I will reveal how to get hired in two weeks or less when applying for work at construction sites. Determine how far you should travel when seeking employment and how to get compensated for traveling expenses. In Discrimination in the Industry we uncover how racially motivated politics is used to exclude blacks and minorities from management positions in the construction industry.

I will also teach you how to resolve and report racial discrimination directed toward you on job-sites. In Staying Productive, we learn how a high level of energy and production can keep you employed for the long term. In Certifications & Trainings the reader will explore what the difference is between the two and what programs will help advance the worker's career. Preparing for the contractors' exam give the reader a detailed road map and the requirements to prepare to pass the states contractor exam. Continue Learning reviews the learning process and how to continue to ask the right questions and develop a lifelong education plan that will advance your career for years to come. Construction Terms is a glossary of housing terms used in the construction field. Learning and memorizing these terms will give you an inside look at the language used by carpenters and builders in construction. These terms will also allow you to see how building materials and construction applications come together in a construction project. More about the Author is a short bio on how I arrived in the construction field as a carpenter.

# MORE ABOUT THE AUTHOR

I grew up in East San Diego during the 1970s-1980s. This was a high crime area were young black men were more likely to go to jail or prison than to graduate from high school. My mother was a single mom, bless her heart raising three kids by herself. She instilled in me at a young age the value of being independent, hard work, and being self-reliant. I ran with a gang in East San Diego and ended up selling drugs and getting addicted to crack cocaine when it was an epidemic in the black communities in the 1980s. Then in 1990 I was sent to prison for three years for a possession of sale of a controlled substance. During my stay in prison I was determined to change my life and re-invent myself. I began to self-educate myself in black history and accounting. I also enrolled in the prisons Amity program one of the best decisions I could have made at that time and place, Amity was a behavior modification program that helped to increased my chances of not returning to prison. After my release I stayed in touch with Amity and attended Alcoholics Anonymous 12-step program. After countless rejections of trying to find employment and nearly giving up I landed a job at Taco Bell. This was one of my first legal jobs and helped to keep me busy and staying out of prison. After about a year of employment I found another job at 7-11 convenient stores. I worked at 7-11 for several years before meeting and marrying my first wife when she became pregnant with my first son Marcus. With the responsibility of having a son being born and he depending on me for his needs I wanted more out of life and sought better employment opportunities. That led me to the field of construction.

# CHAPTER 1

## The Right Mindset

### A Can Do Attitude

*The first thing I recommend you do as a carpenter is dropping the word "can't" from your vocabulary.* We as carpenter and tradesmen get paid for what we **can** do, not what we **can't** do. I remember how, when I was working as an apprentice under the guidance of journeyman carpenters, I would be asked to complete a challenging task and I would view or state that it was impossible to complete the assignment. Then not a few minutes later a journeyman carpenter would complete that same task I had considered impossible. This would always challenge my philosophy and pride, because I insist on always being a competitive person by nature. My thinking has always been: If I can see someone do something, it is conceivable for me to do the same thing. Even today it amazes me what men can accomplish in the construction field when they put their minds to it. I will let you in on a secret. Nothing is impossible. In time, with the right experimentation, training and right minds, anything can be accomplished. The twenty-fifth Nubian black dynasty of Egypt were black men who helped build and expand the great pyramids. These builders were our ancestors and looked just like us. With the right mindset anything is possible.

This is the mindset you must develop and continue to nurture during your construction career. Leaders in this industry are problem solvers. They tackle the difficult projects that others shy away from. This will open the door to opportunities and personal growth. By reading this book you have shown that you are seeking greatness in yourself and your abilities. I congratulate you on this lifelong endeavor. All great men hold one thing in common: the right mindset. They believed in themselves and what they were trying to accomplish and would let nothing stop them from reaching greatness and their full potential. So remember, while going about your daily work as a carpenter, you can achieve anything you set your mind to. Proceed to accomplishing your work with self-determination and careful consideration. Walk the site with high energy and confidence. We represent the men and women of color in the building trades. We take pride in ourselves and our abilities and get to experience the joy of working with our hands. Our ancestors helped build this country's infrastructure, roads, bridges, waterworks and the White House. We build America's future.

## Self-reassurance and Determination

Self-motivation and encouragement must come from within to weather the storms of this trade. I, like so many others at construction jobs, use to look for reassurance and acknowledgement from my employer. This I learned opens the door for frustration and disappointment. I became a workaholic in the attempt to gain praise and self-worth from my employers. Sometimes, this would work in the short term but was not lasting. I would bring this frustration home from work to my wife as anger, bitterness, rage and sadness, sometimes to the point of tears. I don't remember when a change in this thinking occurred or what changed this behavior but I one day realized that it was up to me to encourage myself and give myself praise for work well done. This was a game changer. Then I was no longer always angry and seeking approval from my employers and others. Sometimes I still get joy from hearing others tell me what a great job I have done, but this is unnecessary. Each day I make it a point daily to remind myself that I am a valuable employee giving my best at what I do. There have been many days I was feeling unappreciated and wanted to quit. During these times this is the only thing that kept me going: the faith in myself and abilities as a journeyman carpenter. I re-test my work performance daily. I want to always be at the top of my game and leave in my wake I am a professional and productive worker. If you continue to work like this daily soon the world can't help acknowledging this. This is my sincere belief. You cannot hide greatness and exceptional ability. Continue to give your all, plan your work, and learn something new every day. This is a foolproof plan to greatness in your abilities as a carpenter.

## Giving 110% Daily

Giving your all and then some is difficult to do. I recall watching a movie called *Gattaca* when two brothers were competing to swim out to a buoy out in the bay at night. One brother was believed to be perfect: he was genetically superior to his brother and had everything going in his favor. In spite of all this the other brother won the swimming competition. When ask later how he could accomplish this he stated, "I had saved nothing for the swim back to the shore." This is an example of giving your all for a goal. This brother gave 110% to winning the competition. That's what it takes to stand out from the crowd and this is often what separates the men from the boys and the women from the girls. But many people today hold no idea of what a hard day's work is. Thanks to the construction trade I feel privileged to experience firsthand what this means. There have been days when I felt completely worn out, tired and hungry with no end in sight to that day. This is when I found new strength in myself and abilities as a man and carpenter I did not know existed. Having worked many long hours and weeks, working a regular eight-hour shift almost seems trivial. Sometimes a job will test your physical strength, other times it will test your problem-solving abilities and then at other times test your will power. You must be able to call on any one of these abilities and sometimes all at once to thrive in this industry. Giving your all will cause you to grow in your abilities as a carpenter.

Some days you will love your work, then other days you might hate your job. But just like in life you must learn to accept the good with the bad. I have even grown to respect the bad days because they make the good ones seem so much sweeter. Whatever task is assigned to you give it your best effort and all you can. From sweeping and area to framing a house, they all have importance and value in the greater scheme of the project. If I have to sweep an area I make sure you can eat off the floor when I'm done. I want others to eye that area and say, "He is one hell of a sweeper." Do you get the idea? If I'm building forms for concrete, I want them to say, "Damn, them are good looking forms that will not move when we pour concrete." If I'm framing a house, I want them to say, "That is a class-A framing job." Remember, all work is important and reflects you and our trade as a whole. You should always strive to add value to any company you work for. This is the new era we are living in. The man or woman who continues to add exceptional value as an employee will always have plenty of work.

Whatever you put into your work and profession you will get back. Work with this always in mind. Never do a halfway job when you have the ability and time to complete a job the right way. Always give your best effort in any task and you will be compensated not only from others but have the priceless sense of doing a job right. This is the key to advancing your abilities and your career.

## High Energy

Construction is a high energy occupation. You must hustle to get things done. As a carpenter you must also be able to maintain this level of energy from eight to sometimes 14-hour days. Just go visit any construction site and sit and watch for a short period and it will confirm that statement of high energy. If you are like me, you will want to know what is with all the rushing to get things done. When I was new to the trade I did not get all this at once. The reason is most contractors are under tight schedules to complete a project. They work on a bonus or penalty system that rewards them if they finish a project early and fines them daily when a project goes beyond a completion date. That's one of the main reasons you see the push to get a project completed on most commercial construction sites. We live in a very competitive world today and you must continue to exceed people's expectations to compete in construction and any other occupation. Breaking it down to the individual level as a carpenter, if the contractor you work for does not make money on a project, you suffer a good possibility of getting laid off, so it is in everyone's benefit to hustle and get the project completed in a timely matter. Keep this in the front of you mind when foreman and superintendents bark orders at you and don't take it personal: it's just how things work in this trade.

## My Definition of a Carpenter

A carpenter is a highly skilled worker who takes great pride in himself and his work. He acts in a professional manner when dealing with the public at large and contractors he is employed for. They know that working in a safe and productive manner is the lifeblood of our trade. They cut no corners for quality of work. A carpenter continually seeks to better themselves and their skill in the industry by keeping up-to-date with new materials and construction procedures in the industry. Carpenters invest in their education and construction knowledge by taking continuing vocational classes and hold a library of reference books they can refer to about a task. Tradesmen know how to research and find information about construction topics on the internet and access YouTube videos to enhance further understanding. Skilled workers are testing themselves and testing their performance to make sure it measures up or exceeds the industry standards. Carpenters live a balanced life by not becoming consumed with work and becoming workaholics. They prize family time and core values, and are always ready to help a fellow carpenter regardless of color or race and give back to the community.

## Working Safe

Construction is a dangerous occupation. We are afflicted with one of the highest mortality rates of all lines of work. Working safe and returning home must always be at the forefront of your thinking during your day's work. I have witnessed firsthand what cutting corners in safety can do to workers and their families. Don't become a statistic. I think safety is everyone's job. I don't know about you but I like my fingers, arms, legs and hands and plan to keep all of them in working order. My family is depending on me and I can't make a living in this trade if I end up losing an arm or any fingers or limbs. Many carpenters view safety as a hassle or an unnecessary burden. The bottom line is that safety rules and regulation are in place to protect us the workers.

**Worker Landing Joist for Deck**

Carpenters are often caught up in a dilemma of production versus safety, when this should not be the case. Every tradesman at one time has cut corners because we thought something bad couldn't happen to us. We assume accidents always happen to others and never ourselves. The truth is anyone can get hurt and even worse if we don't take safety seriously and protect ourselves by working safe. Most companies have a safety orientation training after employment and before being permitted to work out in the field. This is for their and your protection to make sure you understand safety procedures of their company and the job-site; take advantage of these trainings and ask questions about anything you do not understand. You must learn to be proactive for your personal safety. It is the contractor's responsibility to provide PPEs, an acronym for personal protective equipment. Your responsibility is to care for and use your PPEs while working. It is also the contractor's responsibility to provide a safe working environment. Do no task or job you feel could injure yourself or others even if asked to by your foreman. Bring any unsafe practices or jobs to your foreman or superintendent ASAP. If you walk in the job-site and see an unsafe condition take care of it on the spot or report it immediately to your supervisor. When working with an apprentice, laborer or another carpenter, always consider their safety and your own. If you see someone working in an unsafe manner tell them about it in a way that is not offensive. Always respect red danger tape by not crossing over or through the tape. This is put up to alert you of a hazardous condition that can cause serious injury or death. When coming to an area with yellow caution tape proceed with caution and extra care. Always test your environment and make sure it's safe before proceeding to any marked tape area. Inspect your safety harness and safety equipment every day. Look for discoloration for tearing in safety harnesses; if you see any such condition discontinue the use. Never enter a confined space marked without notifying the general contractor (GC) on the project.

## An Honest Day's Work for an Honest Day's Pay

Construction is hard work, period. If you have any second thoughts about working hard you should consider entering another profession. Depending on how many hours you work per year in Southern California you could earn between $50,000 to $100,000 per year. What other occupation gives someone without a college degree the opportunity to earn that type of money? We earn a lot of money because a lot is expected in the quality of our work and high production schedule we meet for the general contractor. In the Carpenters Union there is a saying, "An honest day's work for an honest day's pay." What that means is our work effort, or quality of work and production should equal or exceed the pay we receive. It's a feeling that can't be put into words in my honest opinion you get knowing you worked for and deserve every last cent you received on your paycheck. It's the pride of being a carpenter to know that you with your skills and own two hands can provide for your family's needs and wants. We work very hard for our money; we are the back bone of this country—the working middle class. Carpenters through our work are building the infrastructure of this great nation. Knowing you earn and deserve every cent we receive, work hard and be proud.

## Quality Work Matters

Quality seems to have lost its importance in our society. The world has become much smaller and the competition to win construction bids and projects is now global. Just what does that mean for you and me as carpenters? We must continue to strive to always deliver the highest quality product for the company and contractors we work for to remain competitive on a local and global scale. When the companies we work for remain competitive we benefit by being able to remain employed. This is a win/win situation for us and the contractor. Carpenters who perfect their skills and deliver a high-quality product will always be in demand. Sometimes this means spending extra time on a project to make sure the result is right, other times it means to slow down and focus on the task at hand, so everything is right the first time. Whatever the case you must want to deliver a high-quality product you can stand by. Remember, your work reflects your work ethics and values. I have often heard the phrase "signed off on it." As a carpenter that means I can stand by my work and be assured it will pass the highest standards and inspection. This separates the exceptional carpenter from the ordinary carpenter. Always think about quality when performing the task. Quality work always matters.

## Let Nothing Stop You

Being successful in the construction industry is hard work. There are no short cuts. One of the biggest obstacles you will need to overcome is your opinion of yourself and others' view of you and your abilities. I believe anyone with enough determination can accomplish anything in this field. You will be tested by others and most importantly by yourself. There is prejudice and racism in this trade. Don't be misled into thinking it doesn't happen. I had to tolerate this many times myself but I didn't let it stop me. I knew when I first got in this trade I would be a journeyman carpenter. Nothing would take that from me. This is often what it takes: working with difficult foreman and superintendents who don't like you from day one; people who will try to make your workday a living hell. I must inform you this happens not only in the construction field but also other careers. Don't let people with personal issues, prejudices, and outdated views of you and the world stop you. They're not worth it! Remind yourself of this daily. When it comes down to it no one has the power to stop you except yourself. This may be hard to face but it's true. I am thankful for all the foreman and superintendents that made my road to becoming a carpenter hard and challenging. What they thought would stop me empowered me and helped build character. I became a much better skilled worker than if the road I had to travel had been easy. I often smile when I reflect if they only knew how far I had come and that their plans to discourage me backfired and made me a better carpenter. That is the ultimate victory.

## Helping Others

Have you ever heard of the saying, "I am my brother's keeper"? I believe that it's my responsibility to help my fellow carpenters apprentices when needed. When I was an apprentice I was always asking questions and trying to learn all I could about construction. Now I am a journeymen carpenter it's my responsibility to pass this knowledge on to my fellow apprentices especially young black men and minorities in this trade. The reason my focus is on helping my race first is a natural and common sense approach. Being black, I feel I need to help myself and race first before helping others. This should not shock the reader. This is what all other people of different colors do. Another basic and common sense principle of life is you can't help others until you have helped yourself. Let's make clear one point: I am not a racist. I have many friends from all nationalities. Many of them supported me along the way. To them I give my sincere thanks. It is the colored worker who needs most of my help and guidance, and that is why this book was written and why I feel it is so important. I will help any worker who approaches me for help regardless of race and color, but I give special attention to the colored and minority worker who is often a loner on most job-sites. In Southern California there are few black carpenters on job-sites. This is what I know for a fact. We need more young black men entering the trade of construction. For reasons unknown there are few of us out in the field. I hope this book will help inspire and pave the way for more young black men and women considering construction as a career choice. If this book only accomplishes that I would be more than grateful and payed in full for all my efforts. This is my sincere wish. We as a people strive for greatness and open the doors for other black carpenters and tradesmen.

# CHAPTER 2

---

## The Black Contractors
## Association (BCA)

### Introduction to the BCA

Black Contractors Association of San Diego.

The goal of the apprenticeship training facility is to train, and educate and assist tradesmen, contractors and women.

The Black Contractors Association's distinctive qualities are to assist in developing, supporting and helping develop ideas.

They make policies to increase educational opportunities for the entire black community and will help in financial equality.

The BCA's main purpose is to encourage the preservation of the BCA's heritage and creation of the atmosphere that encourages pride.

They help facilitate and seek support for education in the construction field, and also encourage the access of education to all people.

The Black Contractors Association of San Diego establishes networks with the community.

---

## BCA's Apprenticeship Training Center

Is a 10,000 square foot building developed and designed to push inner-city youths into the construction industry? This new state of the art facility provides classroom and shop lab hands-on training. Apprentices must be state certified to attend the classes. This means the contractor has to sponsor him or her into the apprenticeship program.

## The History of The BCA

The Black Contractors Association of San Diego was founded in 1982 as a community based building trade association organized to promote equal opportunity for blacks in construction.

The BCA was given 1,500,000 dollars to the community development block grant program from the city of San Diego, which was started and directed by Abdur-Rahim Hameed, founder and executive president. The request of brick and mortar funding was granted by the city councilman George L. Stevens, who drew support from some of his colleagues in the city council.

The grant was used to build a 10,000 square foot apprenticeship training center for San Diego's inner-city youth and in support of the needs of training the unskilled. The future is bright for the small emerging contracting community who have built solid relationships in the construction industry over the past 25 years working with governmental agencies and politicians.

## Programs Offered by the Black Contractors Association

### Labor Boot Camp

This is a 480-hour tradition program designed to provide hands-on labor training for people who might want to be in construction. It gives them an inside look into what it might take to be a construction worker.

## Labor Boot Camp and ICLP

Subsidized by the building industry, this is a nonprofit labor temp service. They provide workers' compensation, drug screening, and pay off federal and state income and payroll taxes.

## The Inner-City Community Labor Pool

This was established in 1995 to provide skilled labor of all trades to BCA member contractors in the construction industry at large. There were some concerns regarding equal employment opportunities for African Americans in the construction industry. Nevertheless, the labor pool has put over 2500 people to work in the construction field.

# The National Black Contractors Association Mission

Honest appraisal and opinion as they seek to serve as a national voice for the Black Contractors Association chapters across America and to address the needs of African Americans, women and other under-represented groups in construction. It is their mission to provide leadership at the national and state level for African American contractors and all minorities who are builders and laborers who historically have not received a fair share of public and private contract and opportunities. They are committed to providing professional development opportunities, information and trends in the building industry, and programs and services all from the perspective of black contractors and our growth in the industry.

They are committed to assisting the Black Contractor Associations and its members to grow in the following areas:

- Establishing themselves as a one stop all-in-one professional association
- Bringing about economic development that leads to business growth
- Support and promote the advancement of "up and coming" black contractors

Industry News

The National Black Contractors Association (NBCA) is a participant in the Neighborhood Stabilization Program (NSP) to create affordable housing and small business development in urban communities. The Neighborhood Stabilization Program (NSP) was established for the purpose of stabilizing communities that have suffered from foreclosures and abandonment.

About the NBCA

The aim of the National Black Contractors Association is to be a unified association that speaks with one voice on national concerns where inequities and the perception of discrimination is apparent in public and private contracting for African American contractors. Publicly funded projects are mandated to promote equal opportunity for qualified, ready professional building contractors who meet local city, county, state and national standards under the jurisdiction of the state that receives funding through federal and state taxation. The NBCA is positioned to provide national collective leadership to lobby government and state political leaders to uphold and make changes where necessary to improve the quality of life for all citizens of America. Private corporate America has a moral obligation to promote and support equity in hiring, training, and contracting when depending on public support or doing business with the public in any way, shape, fashion or form, as a good corporate citizen.

The NBCA through its national affiliate chapters prepares its members through free online educational training, workshops, mentoring and professional business networking mixers. Introducing professionals to professionals has long been a tool of successful relationship building and trust where individuals are concerned. It helps you to understand the culture of the company or corporation you are seeking to do business with, through knowing and understanding the person or persons in charge.

## Federal Government Links

Department of Labor (DOL)

Department of Transportation Occupational and Health Administration (OSHA)

Office of Small and Disadvantaged Business Utilization (OSDBU)

Small Business Administration

SBA Women's Business Center

SBA Pro-NET

## State of California Government Links

California State Contractors Register

Contractors State Licensing Board (CSLB)

Office of Small Business Certification and Resources (OSBCR)

State of California DVBE referral list

# CHAPTER 3

---

## Apprenticeships

The rest of this book is about gaining the knowledge and skill of becoming a carpenter, something I have spent over the past 20 years perfecting. I can teach to you what I know if you are ready and willing to learn and follow my suggestions. Only time and practice can teach you the hands-on skills you need to succeed out in the field. You must want to be one of the best carpenters in the field. No person or book can give you that. I have always been very competitive and felt the need to prove myself. Motivation must come from deep within. This is what will carry you through the days of wanting to give up or quit. The days of not being praised for your contributions as a skilled worker on the job-site. The times of being passed up for promotions and advancement because of your skin color or race. Let's be real, the world is not a fair place. Don't let this or anyone block you from pursuing your dreams of being a carpenter. So where do you learn and gain the knowledge and experience of becoming a journeyman carpenter? If you possess no experience in construction I recommend joining a carpenter apprenticeship program.

Your next question is, just what is an apprenticeship and how can it help you become a skilled worker? Carpenter apprenticeships are set up to teach someone under the guidance of a journeyman carpenter the practical skills and knowledge of carpentry. Companies and the state where the apprenticeship are set up retain a board of directors who come together to establish training standards for the journeyman carpenters by talking to companies and finding out what skill set is needed to perform carpentry work now and for the future in the construction industry. After completion of a trade school, usually four years of class curriculum and a set hours of hands-on experience under the guidance of a sponsoring company, the state of industry training will award the apprentice a certificate of apprenticeship completion. Depending on if you work for union or non-union companies, there are three different class curriculums of study you must take, and also pass. One is Associated General Contractors of America (AGC), which is the training center for carpenters who go through non-union companies to complete their apprenticeship training. The other is The United Brotherhood of Carpenters. Third is The Black Contractors Association.

**The United Brotherhood of Carpenters**

The United Brotherhood of Carpenters local #547 San Diego has a class curriculum that is offered to apprenticeship members along with out in the field experience to certify and help prepare you to achieve journeyman skills. Another choice is the Black Contractors Association. They have a state certified state of the art training facility that focuses on training inner-city youth the skills required to thrive and compete as a master builder and carpenter. I recommend the Black Contractors Association (BCA) training for young black men, because they offer a unique perspective as to the discrimination policies that black carpenters and contractors must face.

# CHAPTER 4

## Staying healthy and avoiding

## injuries in construction

Gone are the days when companies hired tradesmen with little or no regard for the worker's safety and welfare. A combination of three major forces helped to bring about this improvement in working conditions: the creation of unions to represent the interest of the workers; the creation of the Occupational Safety & Health Administration (OSHA) to police the construction industry, by setting guidelines and regulations that employers must meet to protect employee's safety while working; and new laws being passed by national and local government bodies to ensure that workers have a safe working environment while earning a living. This was due to countless men losing their lives at construction projects and job-sites. Tradesmen and non-skilled labor has all benefited. Today millions of dollars are spent on implementing safety programs and practices on job-sites to ensure workers' safety. Companies also provide workers with the PPE's needed for their job tasks.

Staying healthy and avoiding injuries in construction is the focus of this chapter. Safety is everyone's business on the job-site. Many large companies have a full time employee dedicated to seeing that workers are following the company's safety practices and procedures. Every employee should care about safety. It's our lives and the lives of our fellow employees on the line. Nobody will care as much about you as you yourself will do. That's the bottom line. When you are walking the job-site and see someone working in an unsafe manner or you notice something that can hurt or injure another worker, stop and take the time to tell them the safe way of completing the task or fix the problem yourself. If you are unsure, bring it to the attention of your foreman ASAP.

## Hard Hats

One of the first PPE's developed to protect workers from head injuries was the hard hat. The history of the hard hat dates back to World War I when a company sold hats made of leather. A war veteran after returning home with a steel helmet provided him with ideas to improve industrial safety. In 1919 Bullard patented a hard-boiled hat made of steamed canvas, glue and black paint. When they first were developed there was no standardization. Today performance criteria for head protection are provided for by the American National Standards Institute (ANSA). Hard hats can be purchased in an assortment of colors and designs. Most are made from thermoplastics or fiberglass resin. I can't begin to count how many times wearing my hard hat has protected me from serious head injury. It only takes becoming complacent one time to sustain a life-threatening injury or even worse. Construction sites are full of hazards. Head injuries can be prevented by always wearing your hard hat on the job-site.

## Markings

According to the ANSI/ISEA standard, hard hats must also contain user information such as instructions pertaining to the sizing, care and service life guidelines. Every hard hat conforming to the requirements of ANSI Z89. 1-2014 must be appropriately marked to verify its compliance. The following information must be marked inside the hard hat:

- The manufacturer's name or identifying mark
- Date of manufacture
- The legend, "ANSI Z89. 1-2014"
- The type and class designation
- The approximate head size range

## Safety Glasses

It wasn't until the 1880s that an eye protector patent was issued to *P. Johnson, an African American inventor.* Since then many improvements have been made to the design and function of safety glasses. Eye protection help to protect your eyes while working. Protective equipment only works if you use it. Countless tradesmen suffer from vision loss because of eye injuries and not wearing eye protection. The sad thing is these injuries could have been prevented. Don't become the next statistic. Today's safety glasses come in many designs, shapes and shades. They produce clear glasses for when working in poorly lighted areas, and dark shades for working in direct sun. They also come in many price ranges, from cheap to expensive. Whatever pair of glasses you decide on wearing at the job-site just make sure you always have them on while working. I keep two pairs with me at all times, one clear and one shaded. That way if I'm called to work in a poorly lighted area or in direct sunlight, I am prepared to always ensure my eyes are protected.

## Work Gloves

Just like other forms of personal protective equipment, work gloves help prevent injuries. Carpenters rely on their hands to help them perform skilled work and provide for their families. As a carpenter your hands are one of your most valuable tools. Unlike the tools that can be replaced if damage by running to re-purchase at the nearest Home Depot, your hands are a one of a kind tool that are priceless. Treat them as such. Just like if you had to purchase a tool that was a large investment and could not be replaced, you should value your hands even more. Work gloves come in many materials and sizes tailored for the job to be performed. They make thick rubber gloves to protect your hand against concrete and chemical burns. They have heavy Knoxville Double Palm Gauntlet gloves for ironworkers. Carpenters wear a palm flex thin material glove to allow for fingering nails. Some carpenter gloves come with some fingertips already removed. There are countless others specialty gloves designed to protect your hands depending on the work being done. There have been many situations when someone working on a job-site received what appeared to be a small insignificant cut or injury to the hand that later developed into something that required major medical attention. These type of injuries can often be eliminated by always wearing protective work gloves while working.

## Hearing Protection

Hearing protectors reduce the noise exposure level and the risk of hearing loss. According to OSHA people should wear a hearing protector if the noise or sound level at the workplace exceeds 85 decibels. The decibel is a logarithmic unit used to express the ratio of two values of a physical quantity, often power of intensity. Hearing protection choices come in earmuffs and ear plugs, and within these two choices are countless designs and options to choose from. Hearing protection also comes in many price ranges. The noise level you are exposed to should determine the choice of hearing protection you use. There are many sounds and levels of noise you will be constantly exposed to as a carpenter and skilled tradesmen. These sounds come from the many types of tools and machinery needed to complete a building from start to finish. You must be ready to protect yourself from permanent hearing loss by this exposure. Many carpenters after working years in the construction field suffer hearing loss. In many of these cases hearing loss could have been prevented by using hearing protection. Your hearing allows you to experience and enjoy life with your loved ones and family. Protect your hearing.

## Face Shields

Protect workers from injury to their eyes and face. They add an extra layer of protection and go beyond the standard protection of eyeglasses. Carpenters or tradesmen working with a grinder or chop saw with a metal blade should be always wearing a face shield. When grinding or cutting metal, fine particles of metal shavings can become airborne and penetrate beyond the protection of safety glasses. Welding and joining metal or cutting steel with cutting torches create an intense bright light that can damage the eyes. Welders use a face shield with a special lens to protect the eyes from the brilliant light created due to the intense heat needed to bring steel to its melting point. Face shields are also used to protect workers from burns and flying debris or particles. Face shields come in many designs and functions tailored to the job or task that needs to be completed. The rule of thumb is if grinding, welding, or cutting metal a face shield should be worn. Check with your foreman if unsure about the proper use.

## Preventing Tendon and Joint Injury

Many carpenters who have been working years in the trade suffer from joint, nerve and tendon damage. When I was a carpenter apprentice many journeyman carpenters who had been in the trade for years told me about the damage to joints over the years that construction causes, but I was young then and thought this could never happen to me. This is a real health issue that many construction workers may have to face one day due to the high demands placed on their bodies. Some of these injuries cannot be eliminated due to striking metal or driving nails with a hammer over an extended period, or operating a 90lb jack hammer in concrete demolition work over extended periods of time. There are many things in your control as a worker that can lessen or at least reduce the impact of these type of injuries over your working career. My first suggestion is not to purchase hammers with metal handles. These type of hammers do nothing to help absorb the shock impact on joints, tendons and nerves. Wood handles offer a much better choice for protecting against shock impact and continual vibrations when striking hard surfaces. My second suggestion is to purchase a high-quality elbow sleeve like Copper Fit to help protect your joints from damage. I have been in the trade for over twenty years and often when just relaxing have to deal with sharp continuous pain due to damage to my joints. I'm writing this section so you can learn from my mistakes.

## Avoiding Back Injuries

We take a lot of things for granted in this life when we're young. One of them is a good strong back that is pain free. Have you ever heard the saying, "You never miss the well until it runs dry"? The same can be said about being in good health with a strong back. I never appreciated this until I became complacent on a job-site with Morley Builders at the San Diego Pacific Beacon Project in 2008. The task I was performing that day did not take a lot of thinking—or maybe it should have, now thinking back to that day. Some other workers and I were lifting poll shores from one level to the next. I was the man on the top level lifting and stacking the poll shores on carts with wheels. Sounds simple enough, you would think. The big mistake I made was pulling them up and making a twisting motion while tossing the poll shores on the carts. This continued for several hours with no problems, when suddenly my back seized and went into repeated spasms. I can't put into words the pain I was in. I had to be taken to urgent care. After x-rays and exams by a physician I was told that I had compressed the disk in my back and that it might require surgery. It took three months of physical therapy and working light duty before I could return to my normal work routine. Not even to mention the unbearable pain and back spasms I had to suffer. The moral of this story is that the way we do small things is crucial to helping prevent major injuries. Had I stopped to consider shifting my body instead of twisting my back, this injury could have been avoided. This was a painful lesson learned.

Carpenters and tradesmen need good strong backs to perform the daily work and job assignments given to us. With a major back injury, we can be put out of the construction game. We could lose the ability to work and provide for our families. This could be a game changer, and not in a good way. When lifting something heavy on the job-site, always bend your knees and lift with your legs, not your back. If material is too heavy for you to lift, get help from a co-worker. Better to avoid injury and work another day than try to prove how strong you are. Always shift your body instead of twisting your back when stacking material. Purchase and use a good back brace if your work requires lifting heavy objects for extended periods of time. Remember, being a carpenter often requires working smarter, not harder. By following these simple rules, you can avoid many back injuries and ensure a long healthy career as a carpenter.

## Face Respirators and Dust Mask.

Construction sites are full of hazards you must protect yourself from: dust particles, harmful fumes and gases, smoke and vapors. Many men and women in the construction industry have lost their lives due to these hazards. Wearing the right face respirator or dust mask is your first line of protection against these health hazards.

A respirator or dust mask should be provided by the employer in the control of occupational diseases caused by breathing air contaminated with harmful dust, fogs, fumes, mist, gases, smokes, or vapors. Their primary objective is to prevent atmospheric contamination.

It is your responsibility to use these forms of breathing protection when you are exposed to these contaminants. First, you should become familiar with the different types of face respirators and dust mask so you will choose the one that will provide the most protection when you have to work in an area that will put you at risk. Ask your employer if they provide trainings to workers in the proper use of these PPEs. Only after proper training on their correct use should you wear and be exposed in areas with breathing protection is required.

## Fall Protection and Body Harnesses

There are two systems used to protect workers from falls. The first one we will talk about is fall protection. These systems when used correctly must prevent workers from falling. Hand rails are an example of one of these systems. Job-site hand rails must be built to a certain OSHA job-site code compliance. Bottom rail height should be 21 inches to the top. The top rail should be 42 inches to the top. If 2 x 4 is used for railing, 16 sinkers must be used to prevent hand cuts and injuries. Hand rail should also be constructed to withstand 200lb of force when applied. This is a fall protection system designed to protect workers from fall hazards. Floor openings that are covered are another example of a fall protection system in use. These are just two examples. Next we will discuss fall arrest systems. They are engineered to slow the rate of fall and prevent workers from falling over a certain distance. Body harnesses are one component of these systems. Nano locks, lanyards and retractable life lines are other parts of this system with anchor points completing this system. These are just some examples of a fall arrest system. There are many others.

Commercial and residential carpenters are both exposed to fall hazards. To protect workers from injuries due to falls the OSHA has many guidelines and regulations that employers must follow on job-sites. One is the leading edge rule in commercial deck construction. Workers must wear body harnesses when working 6 feet or less off the leading edge of a deck where there is a fall hazard. OSHA also stipulates that fall protection must be worn when a worker is exposed to a fall greater than 6 feet even when working off a ladder.

Everyone wants to return home after a work day. No one plans on having a fatal fall during the work day, but they do happen all over the country. Some workers view wearing safety equipment as a hassle they can do without. Only after hearing about or witnessing a fatality do some workers wake up to the fact that men and women lose their lives in this trade when safety rules and procedures are not followed. How would your family and loved ones support themselves if you did not return home after a fatal fall? Safety starts with the right mindset. Safety rules and regulations are designed to protect us all so we can return to our families at the end of the day.

# CHAPTER 5

## Union versus Non-union

First, there are good and bad points that can be made for belonging to the United Brotherhood of Carpenters or the Associated General Contractors of America. I have worked for both organizations. I'm not and have never been a board member for either of these organizations and have no hidden agenda in pushing or endorsing one or the other. So I'm going to tell it like it is without sugar coating any information of my honest opinion on this subject.

### Contractor Specialties

One thing I like about working for general contractors or the GC is that you get the chance to learn and do everything from grading for the foundation work to caulking windows and the punch list. The reason I say this is that when you work with concrete specialty companies in San Diego, 96% of the time you are doing concrete formwork only. When I started in the trade back in the 1990s I began my apprenticeship with a company called Soltec Pacific, a general contractor (GC). I did not realize how very fortunate I was at the time to be working with a company that exposed me to and let me gain experience in almost all facets of construction from the ground up. This is one reason I know how to do grade work for concrete, how to operate a wide range of equipment, how to frame walls and so on. Since I completed my apprenticeship and worked for the Carpenters Union, almost all the work I experienced has been concrete forms.

Union companies' main specialty is concrete. Local #547, the Carpenters Union in San Diego, has a monthly list of union companies like JT Wimsatt, JR Concrete, McCarthy Builders, Bomel Construction, and Webcore Builders who bid on concrete projects. Their specialty is parking structures, high-rise hotels and commercial buildings. Some union companies like Skanska and Disney Construction, which is based out of northern California, do bridge work and major dam projects. They are the concrete sub-contractors for the general contractors who are non-union companies in San Diego. You can learn a lot with any one of these companies but concrete is only the foundation or structure part of a building and only one part in the total construction process. The more you know in this trade and the more experience you can gain in many areas of construction the more valuable you are as an employee. So if you are seeking a wide range of experience and want to be exposed to the complete construction process, union concrete specialty companies will not be a good fit in accomplishing this goal. On the plus side, what I love about union companies is the huge concrete projects they work on. Union carpenters are some of the most productive and skilled carpenters in this area. Concrete is what the union does best and in this area it is second to none.

Non-union companies like Soltek Pacific, Davis & Reed, Kitchell, Swinerton Builders and RA Burch are the general contractors at the job-site and oversee the project from beginning to end, allowing you as a carpenter to learn many more aspects and get to be involved in many more areas of the project. As a carpenter apprentice I think companies like these will give you the greatest opportunity to learn and be exposed to the building schedules from the ground up. These companies use some of the construction trades most rounded or multi-skilled carpenters. Many of them can operate heavy equipment, lay-out buildings, finish concrete, hang drywall and install windows and doors. Non-union companies that act as GCs hire all the sub contractors and oversee all the activities until the project's completion. They rarely have a specialty even though many have their own concrete divisions, framers, and finish carpenters to help complete a project.

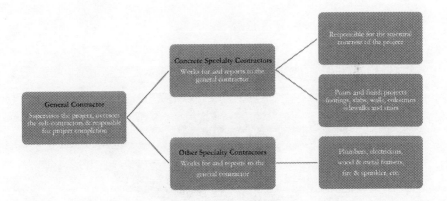

**General Contractor & Sub-Contractor Responsibility Flow Chart**

## Discrimination Practices

Job discrimination happens in union and non-union companies. This has been my personal experience. It may be worse in union companies where membership in San Diego union hall is about 80%–90% Latino or Mexican workers. I am just stating the facts. After being in the trade for about 20 years, I would estimate that black carpenters make up only about 2%–3%, if that. That's why I feel in my heart and soul that writing this book is so very important. Black Men and women should seek better-paying jobs in construction. Booker T Washington, the founder of the Tuskegee University, saw the value of our race getting education in the trades. We can't always be pointing the finger at companies and just wishing they would give us more opportunities. As young and older black men and women we need to claim our fair share of these good paying jobs.

If companies refuse to give us the opportunity to prove ourselves then we need to start our own construction companies that will give young black men and women, these financial income opportunities to escape poverty and join the working middle class. Every race seems to be doing this except our own, with a few exceptions to this rule. Only after we start creating our own businesses in construction as contractors will we be in a position to lift ourselves and other young black people up onto a somewhat level playing field. The reason I didn't say level is because even black contractors face discrimination when bidding for work, but are in a better position to help themselves and others. I think this is the best solution and approach to the discrimination issue.

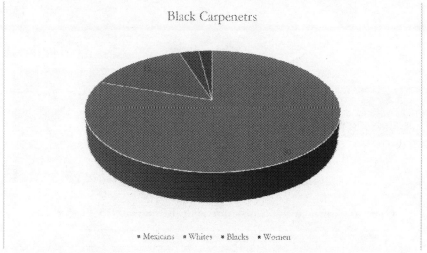

Black Carpenetrs

* Mexicans * Whites * Blacks * Women

**Percentage of Black, White, Mexicans and women carpenters in the union**

I have written a section about what it takes to get your contractor's license. Please pursue this if this is your dream. The black community and youth needs you. You can also find more detailed information about the requirements on this subject by visiting the Contractors State Licensing Board's website at www Cslb. ca.gov . It is much better in my honest opinion to bid your own work and become a licensed contractor than work for contractors who won't give you the chance to compete on a fair playing field. Once you become a licensed contractor you will hold the honor and opportunity to help another black apprentice learn a trade, make good money and provide for their family. This is the greatest contribution you can make to the construction field for our people. I don't mean to rain on your parade but job discrimination has been going on since the Civil War when they didn't pay black soldiers the same as white. Since the Civil Rights marches in the 1960s things have gotten better but we are a long way from being valued and treated equal in the job market, construction or otherwise. Union and non-union companies don't mind giving a few blacks jobs—hell, it even makes them look good in their public relation campaigns. Then when someone asks if they have any minorities working for them they can happily call out the names of the few black employees they employ. What I'm talking about is job promotions and the responsibilities to run and manage work crews and projects. This is where the pavement meets the road and where most companies fall way short. There is a handful of blacks in these positions but nowhere near what the numbers should be at.

## Swearing In

There is another major difference when joining the Carpenters Union and that is the swearing in ceremony. Anyone who joins the union must take the oath that states you will uphold all the bylaws of the Carpenters Union including not working for non-union companies or crossing strike lines that union members may have if they feel members are being treated unfairly. You must swear on your honor as a person that you will support the union and all its activities. This is a big deal so don't take it lightly. If you are found guilty of violating union laws, you can be brought up on charges by the board members and expelled from the union depending on the charges and end up losing all your union benefits like health coverage for you and your family and pension retirement. Non-union organizations like the Associated General Contractors of America do not swear an oath for its members, or at least there were none when I was an active member. With the AGC you can look and find work at any construction project when times get slow out of the organization without the repercussion of being brought up on charges an being kicked out. This is an immense difference and something that should be carefully evaluated before taking the oath to become a member and join the United Brotherhood of Carpenters or better known as the Carpenters Union.

## Union Meetings

Meetings for local Carpenters Union #547 San Diego are held monthly on the third Thursday of each month and are a great place to find out where the latest construction projects are and who is doing the hiring.

They often have the inside scoop for upcoming project like foreman and superintendent contact information, and job access to aid union members in their job search. Union meetings also have the latest job search list that has all the union companies that are working, hiring or about to start new projects in the coming months. They also swear in new members and talk about relevant issues facing the union. Here you can talk and meet other carpenters and make new networking connections that can aid you in your job search. They often also have pizza and drinks with free T-shirts and tool giveaways. Union meetings offer a great way to network with other carpenters and build relationships that can be mutually beneficial in finding work or getting job-site information.

## Work Hours

Union companies are notorious for working long hours. Most union projects are under great pressure for completion dates and hire many workers at the beginning of the project. This push continues, many times working 10 to 12-hour days until they reach a point in the job where the floors will become a typical height. The hotel lobby's main entrance and commercial buildings often require a high deck. This concrete deck is 12 feet or greater, which takes a tremendous amount of manpower and dollars to accomplish. Once they reach the typical deck height, manpower is cut to a small crew, layoffs are given out to workers and the small crew of carpenters is kept on to completing the building.

## Union Layoffs

One thing I have noticed about being a union carpenter is there are constant layoffs. Most building projects are short term: six months to a year, with a good run being one to two years. The money you make as a union carpenters is good, but the work is unsteady so you must plan accordingly. This is especially true for black carpenters who are usually the last hired and are the first laid off. A smart union carpenter is always looking for his next job or project. Job layoffs are just part of being a union carpenter. Networking becomes a necessity. Keep up with the latest project developments, where the cranes are, where the job-sites are, and who is doing the hiring. The rollercoaster ride of union jobs can make purchasing a home or getting loan difficult due to job instability. The Carpenters Union out of work list is often outdated and repetitive. Many times while searching for employment and referring to the list I notice the same companies were on the previous month's list. Often jobs on the list are put on way too early because the project has not started yet or it's still in the grading phase. The best way to find work by far is by word of mouth. The union list has been helpful but it's just one tool I use to help me find employment. If you want to last in the union, you must be very proactive when job searching. Having your eyes and ears open for the next employment opportunity often becomes second nature. There are few people who have been working for the same union companies for years, but this is often the exception rather than the norm.

# CHAPTER 6

---

# The Tools of the Trade

Quality tools versus cheap tools. Let's start with lesson number one. Your tools are your livelihood and speak a lot about you and how seriously you take your profession. When I started in the trade back in 1996 for a company called Soltek Pacific as a carpenter apprentice, I would buy all the cheapest tools: and gear on sale, bargain tools, tools at yard sales and swap meets. My thinking then was a cheap tool is just as good as any other tool, so why should I waste money on expensive high-quality devices? This was the thinking of someone green as we would say in the field, a newbie to construction. My thinking and purchasing habits when it comes to my working instruments have been revised. My thinking now is that my tools are an extension of me and my skills as a carpenter. In order for me to produce a high-quality product I must purchase the best tools available. Quality tools break less often than cheaper tools, saving labor hours and replacement cost over the long run. Another benefit of making a habit of only buying high-quality instruments is that most of the time they come with lifetime warranties, giving you added peace of mind and an insurance policy when you purchase. There is another benefit often overlooked as well by the black or minority carpenter entering the field, often with less discretional income than their counterparts. Your tools say a lot about you as a skilled tradesman and carpenter and set the first impression job-site foreman and superintendents make of you. Have you ever heard the expression "You never get to make another first impression"? This is true for the black carpenter who is often stereotyped into being less skilled and of less value compared to his White and Mexican counterparts.

**Selecting a pair of carpenter bags.** So what type of carpenter bags should you purchase? I have spent a great deal of money over the last 20 years trying a great number of bags from the cheap to the most expensive. What I recommend for this expensive lesson is to purchase a good set of high-quality Occidentals carpenter bags. A good set of leather or Kevlar bags will cost you about $300. The good thing about purchasing quality bags is that they come with deep pockets to hold your tools securely when climbing over or under forms or crossing over building footings. You can purchase these from White Cap Building Supplies or Tool-Up Building supplies. I'm right handed, so I purchase bags where my lay-out instruments can be accessed from my right bags.

**Hand Tools.** They include my tape measure, speed square, torpedo level, chalk line and reel, plumb bob, and carpenter's pencils. My left bags carry my nails and my cat's paw, a mini pry-bar for pulling nails. The nails I carry are 16Ds' for concrete forms, 16 pennies for wood stud framing, and 8Ds' and 8 pennies for plywood. If you are a union concrete forms carpenter, it is also a good idea to purchase a spud wrench for hardware and lining up holes and a long 12-inch screw driver. These are the basics.

**Specialty Gear.** There are specialty tools such as a building materials' calculator for take-off work and a sledge hammer for driving wood and metal stakes; a quality 4-foot level for checking plum and level; and a good body harness for working heights greater than 6 feet as required by OSHA if working on commercial high-rise projects. One more note on instruments before we move on: the rule of thumb I was taught as an apprentice is to purchase a new tool needed with every paycheck. You will be amazed if you follow this simple suggestion how soon you will build up your tool arsenal. On that note, make sure you never have to borrow another man's gear more than once. This is a sign you need to purchase the tool being borrowed ASAP! I am a big fan of Home Depot, where you can find most of your tools for commercial and residential construction. There are specialty stores that cater to contractors like White Cap and Professional Contractor Supply. If you're running work and are a building contractor, they may be the better choice because their employees are more knowledgeable about contractor's needs and the specialty tools that go along with that.

**Power Tools.** One of the first power tools every good carpenter needs is a good electric saw for rough cutting wood. There are many choices depending on your needs, taste, and budget. There are a few I can recommend after proving their value and durability in the commercial construction field. Skill Saw's a brand I can recommend and is sold at Home Depot and has been used out in the industry by journeyman carpenters for over the last twenty years. This power tool has taken a lot of physical abuse at job-sites such as being dropped, the cord being tugged on and used to pull the tool up ladders, although the manufacture wouldn't recommend this practice. It's almost indestructible. I said almost. The only maintenance that is required is to check and replenish the oil for the motor, which out in the field is rarely done. Sometimes I have had to replace the cord, which you can purchase. What more could you ask for in a tool?

Skill Saw brand also sells the Magnum 77 model that is a much lighter saw for carpenters who do a lot of overheads, vertical, and horizontal cuts when framing houses. Another brand that has recently appeared at commercial projects is De Walt. They have been making quality tools such as tape measures, ladders, cordless tools, and air compressors for over twenty years I know about. The recent appearance of their electric saw in the field has impressed me enough to make it one of only two saws I recommend. I have used it out at job-sites; it's light and has a smooth operation, which makes it a pleasure to work with. Getting back to electric saw basics, the cutting blade can be replaced with specialty blades. For your wood projects you can purchase anything from a rough ripping blades to a fine finish cutting blade with different teeth counts depending on your project needs. You can also purchase diamond blades for cutting concrete. These blades have rough cut industrial diamonds inserted in the blade for cutting concrete. Be very careful when cutting concrete not to over-work the motor on your electric power saw or you could end up burning out the motor. They also sell metal cutting blades used for cutting steel such as rebar, unistrut and all-thread.

Eventually you will need to purchase a good Sawzall for demolition work. The brand I recommend here is Milwaukie. Just like the Skill Saw brands this has been tested and proven its durability and reliability in the commercial construction industry for years. A Sawzall is basically an electric hand saw that moves back and forth at a high rate of speed. This is used in demolition work where the cut need not be accurate. This will cut through almost anything with the right blade. Blades come in different sizes, lengths and teeth counts depending on your project's needs. They are an indispensable tool for cutting through lumber like 2 x 4, and 4 x 4, nail embedded lumber, PVC conduit, metal, plywood, etc. I also recommend that you own at least one with a cord before purchasing a cordless model. The reason behind this is that corded tools need not be charged before and during use. Many demolition projects require countless cutting for hours on end and you want your tool in this example to be hassle free without the added headache of needing to be charged. But some carpenters will argue otherwise, with the recent improvements in cordless battery technology like the lithium 22 volt batteries that are becoming a close competitor to tools with cords.

I also think every carpenter should own an air compressor and nail gun. If space is not a factor in your purchase, I recommend that you purchase one with a double tank. Then you will have all the power you need to drive any nail or staple depending on the project size. Hitachi compressors and nail guns have always been one of my favorite brands. There are many choices and brands to choose from. My advice before purchasing is test a company's tool out in the field and then make your choice based on your experience before your purchase. Having a nail gun will improve your production output for framing projects or wall panel forms. You also can eliminate or reduce a lot of cartilage and nerve damage that comes from swinging a hammer for years. Don't underestimate the importance of this. When I was a young apprentice old time carpenters warned me of the damage to my joints that could happen from swinging the wrong hammer for years. I did not take their advice and now I'm paying the price in joint pain that could have been reduced by changing from metal to a wood or fiberglass handle hammer, or buy purchasing a nail gun and compressor and letting them do the nailing for me. Live and learn. Now you know this, don't let this happen to you.

**Cordless tools**. Eventually you will need to add a cordless tool arsenal. For every kit I have with a cord I have the same tool in a cordless version. The main reason is that cordless outfits give you the ability to work without having a power source nearby or having to carry and un-roll sometimes hundreds of feet of cord to do your work. This can save you time and frustration when you only need to make a few cuts. The new battery operated gizmos sold today are much more powerful than their predecessors of just ten years ago. Also, the new lithium battery technology has allowed the battery life to improve and reduce the size and the weight of the battery and tool. Cordless tools are rivaling the power of instruments with cords as a technology improves. Many of the manufactured brands sell battery operated tools in bundles for greater savings to the consumer. If you purchased a tool in a bundle package your savings will be much more than if you buy the same tool separately, saving yourself hundreds if not thousands of dollars depending on how many tools you purchase.

Some of the brands I recommend in this area are Makita, Milwaukie and De Walt. These tool combos often come with a cordless Sawzall's, Drill Motor, impact driver and flash light, all cordless tools should come with a battery charger and two batteries. The reason you need two batteries is so that one is always charging when one is in use.

Power actuated kits are tools that can shoot different size pins and fasteners into concrete. Ramset is the brand I am most familiar with. Many require class training certifications before you can use them out at the job-site. You must be careful when operating these powerful instruments that can cause great bodily harm and death if used incorrectly or in an unsafe manner. They work in the same way as a gun. They fire shots filled with gun powder that explodes and fires the pin or fastener into the surface material. You are required to keep a pail of water nearby to throw the un-spent shot into to prevent explosions or fire hazards. Most carpenters will yell out, "Fire in the hole!" when discharging a shot so as not to startle other workers who may be nearby. The most common use I am aware of for this tool is to pin down mudsill and bottom plates into a concrete slab. Make sure you are trained and understand how this tool works before making a purchase.

There is many other gear you can purchase depending on what your specialty in the field is and what different jobs call for. The rest of the tools you need can be purchased on an as need basis. Most union companies supply their carpenters with power tools, therefore eliminating the need to bring your own power gear to the job-site. This over the long run can save you hundreds of dollars on wear and tear on tools and replacement cost. This is one benefit of being a union carpenter. Many non-union companies require their carpenters to purchase and provide their own tools. Some non-union companies will replace or reimburse you if your tool becomes damaged or not operational, but it depends on the company and the policies vary from company to company. As a journeyman carpenter or apprentice, tools will or should be an important part of your life and give you the ability to complete your work and make a good living; you will purchase tools for the rest of your career, so take your time and choose wisely.

**Tool Maintenance.** After years in the trade working as a carpenter, you like me will have invested thousands of dollars in hand and power devices. This is not cheap and when all added up can be a major cash investment. Like any other investment you need to take care of them and maintain your tool to receive the greatest return and benefits. How do you take care of your gear? Brand manufactures will often have a small booklet that comes when you purchase hand and power tools. In this situation it is best to follow their guidelines and suggestions. Many times when taking care of power or hand tools it's just a matter of using common sense. First, only use an instrument for what it was designed for. This will not only increase the tool's life but also prevent injuries and sometimes great harm or death.

Some examples are don't use a wrench as a hammer or pry-bar, never use a screw driver as a chisel and so on. Rule number two: don't carry or pull tools up ladders by the cord. This is a common practice by carpenters in the field who are in a rush to get things done. The main reason is that they need to either pull a tool up or lower a tool down a ladder in the process of working. A simple solution to this problem when working off ladders is to always carry a short length of rope with you to tie the tool in a slip-knot when raising or lowering tools up and down ladders. This is an OSHA requirement.

Never cut with a dull blade on any saw. This not only may damage the motor by overworking it but it may cause a kick back which can sever fingers and limbs. If a blade is dull replace it with a new one. Hand tools that are broken, chipped or dull should be repaired, replaced or taken out of service.

Next keep instruments clean, dry and stored in an organized manner when not in use. Many tools can become damaged by just throwing them in the job box at the end of the shift or job assignment. Remember: a damaged tool will not be of any use for you the next day. The time you may think you are saving by just throwing the gear in the box if broken or damaged in the process will cost you time and money the next day to have it repaired or replaced. Also, when you need a tool it's much faster to find it in a clean and organized job box. We make our living by using and depending on quality tools to help us get our job done. Treat all tools like you had to pay for them and like they are your own and you will be less likely to damage them.

**Work Boots.** Okay, now that I have driven home the importance of your work tools let's move on to your work boots. Being a carpenter out in the field you will be required to be on your feet all day or at least for extended periods of time. My recommendation and my experience has taught me to buy the highest quality steel toe boots to protect my feet and provide comfort and durability while working. There are many choices in boots from shoe manufactures like Sears Die Hard and Wolverines. One benefit of purchasing Wolverines is they require no break-in period. They feel comfortable from day one, and believe me that's important when you are up on your feet all day long. Some places of business like Boot World and Sears may offer union carpenters a discount. This is something you should check out when purchasing your next pair, the savings amount to 10% of the purchase price. Also, once a year manufacturers like Sears Die Hard and Wolverines offer sales, sometimes of almost half price, and this is a great time to take advantage and stock up by purchasing two pairs of boots at one time.

**Job Pants**. Now you will need good durable work pants. Another misconception is that any pair of pants will do. That's just not the case. Quality pants will protect your legs from minor cuts and provide comfort during the work-shift. For work pants selection you can't go wrong with Carpenter's jeans. I like them because they come with a hammer holder on the side, pockets for your phone and plenty of other deep pockets perfect for the blue collar working man. I also like Dickeys jeans. They are comfortable and number one for durability along with original Levi's 501.

**Work Trucks**. Now you have your tools, work boots and pants squared away, let's talk transportation. I believe any person who plans on earning a living for an extended amount of time in construction should own or purchase a truck. This is especially true for the black carpenter. I can't tell you all the opportunities that owning a truck has opened for me. My truck serves as an office, work station, and mobile factory. If you are committed to this industry and going to invest in quality tools it only makes sense to own a truck to secure and transport your tools to job-sites and work locations. Let's reflect on what I stated earlier that you only get one chance to make a first impression. If two carpenters seek employment at the same job-site at the same time and one pulls up in a truck with a tool box mounted on his truck and the other pulls up in a Cadillac, who do you think the foreman or superintendent will perceive has the most value as a skilled worker? I'm not saying there is anything wrong with owning a Caddie. Hell, I own one myself.

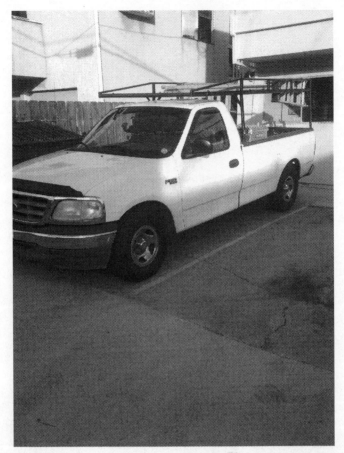

**Basic Work Truck with Mounted Tool Box and Materials Rack**

The point I'm trying to make is that they have no place on a job-site unless you have a white-collar job in the office. As minorities we need every advantage we can get to level the playing field. Save your luxury or sports car for the weekend or off-site activities. The type of truck you own is not that important. Just make sure it's a real work truck pickup and not some Cadillac Escalade that has a bed for carrying groceries. After securing a truck you will want to get a tool box mounted in the bed for securing and transporting your tools.

Now that we have covered all the basic tools, boots, pants and owning a work truck, what do we do? So far, if you have followed my advice you are off to a great start. You have all the basic tools, work clothing and you look like a skilled worker. You are on the fast track to becoming an in demand first-rate carpenter. As minorities we need every advantage we can get or create to level the playing field.

# CHAPTER 7

## Building Materials

### Wood

Wood is a fantastic building material, both strong and flexible. Lumber can withstand great loads and is resilient enough to regain its shape when pressures are removed. Because wood is so useful, it has many names according to its source, sizes, uses, and so on. Wood is defined as hardwoods or soft wood. Almost all construction lumber is soft wood. Names of hardwoods are maple, oak, and walnut. Sheet materials such as plywood and composite board are sold by the square foot, which is length times width; lumber thickness affects price. The manner in which logs are transformed into lumber determines the final size and moisture content of the wood. Wood may also be marked "pressure treated." Such wood, after treatment, may be left exposed to the weather. This is a great building material solution for building fencing, mud sill plates for framing, and other building projects where the wood will be continuously exposed to the outside elements. Pressure treated wood also helps prevent termite damage and wood rot that comes from moisture exposure over long periods of time. Pressure treating is the most effective way to preserve wood; lumber is placed in a closed container, and preservatives are forced in it.

**Vertical structural members** are columns, post, and studs. They are 2 x 4, or 2 x 6 placed 16 in. or 24 in. on-center; the vertical wood members in frame construction. Posts are the major vertical members in a post and beam house. Posts also refer to 4 x 4, or 6 x 6, columns and post transfer weight to the foundation or to concrete pads or footings in the basement. Girders (or carrying timbers), beams, and joists are horizontal structural members. Joist is dimensional lumber set on edge to support flooring or ceilings. Like studs they are spaced at 16 in. or 24 in. on-center. Beams are the horizontal supports in a post and beam house; they are bigger than joists, though not always longer, and are laid on edge for maximum load bearing depth. Girders are the major members of a house, and often support walls and floors above. Like columns they rest on the foundation. Planks and decking are lumber at least 2 in. thick, used as flooring or roof sheathing. In post and beam construction, decking is often tongue-in groove a roofing material or siding that has a protruding lip and a groove or slot in the opposite edge of the material to receive the lip. For greater rigidity resting right on top of the beams, such as decking is both exposed ceiling and flooring above. Rafters, bridging and bracing are members placed diagonally. Rafters support the roofing and are dimensional lumber. Bridging and bracing are often low-grade lumber used to keep structural wood members from twisting and turning; bracing is associated with studs and bridging with joists and rafters. The grade of a wood depends on its strength, imperfections, and sometimes usage.

**Light Steel Framing.** Light steel framing comprises of metal studs set into runner channels, members of the system being joined by sheet metal screws. It is recommended where fire codes are stringent. Although light-weight the system is strong. The structural integrity of metal stud-walls, however, depends on all the members of the system being tied together by sheet material. You may encounter difficulty in using metal studs in renovation and remodeling work. First, they are expensive. Second, they may be incompatible with existing wood framing. Third, because of the way they gain rigidity and strength, they may be impractical where floors are not level.

**Trusses.** Trusses can be fabricated from wood or metal. Besides being strong and relatively light-weight, trusses allow builders to channel ducts, pipes and wiring through open spaces. This can be a great advantage in renovation work.

**Laminated Beams.** For many years used for commercial use, glue laminated beams are found increasingly in residences. Glue-lams, as they are called, are fabricated from relatively short pieces, overlapped or finger joints glued in an appropriate manner, and clamped under great pressure. Glue-lams are expensive, but their stability and strength make them better suited than solid wood in high-load situations such as headers and clear span beams. They are far less likely to warp or cup.

**Plywood.** The strength of plywood is achieved by alternating the wood grain of adjacent plies. Plywood is the most frequently chosen material for sheathing, subflooring and other structural uses. Alternating the grain also avoids the problem of splitting common in solid wood as it expands and contracts. Plywood most commonly comes in 4 ft. by 8 ft. sheets.

**Composite board.** Composite board products are made from wood, but the strength and form of the materials is engineered by man.

**Particle Board**. Particle board is classified by the size of particle and by type, strength, and density. Type I particle board is intended for interior use. Type II has waterproof glue and is intended for exterior use.

**Concrete.** Concrete is a mixture of Portland cement, sand, and aggregate or gravel. The curing period of concrete is 28 days, meaning it takes that amount of time for it to reach full strength. Concrete will take on any form that it is cast in our poured in. This gives this building material great versatility in taking on whatever form the building architect or engineers envision.

# CHAPTER 8

## Fasteners and Connectors

If woods are a universal building material, metal is the universal connector. Nails of many types, screws, and bolts are discussed in this section, as well as specialty plates that reinforce structural members. Nails vary according to length, size of the head, shape of shank, point, and composition.

**Length**. Nails are organized in ("D") sizes: the larger the nail, the greater the penny rating.

**Head.** The shape of a nail's head depends on its use and whether the nail is to be left exposed or to be concealed. Smaller heads such as those for casing, finished, or some kinds of flooring can be easily sunk.

**Shank shapes**. Nail shanks usually have a straight shaft; variations allow greater holding strength. Spiral flooring nails resist popping up. Nails and shorter shank are favored for hardwoods.

**Points.** Nail points usually taper to four-sided points, but there are some variations. Blunt point nails are less likely to split wood; you can make your own by hammering down a nail point.

**Materials and composition**. Most nails are fashioned from medium grade steel. Nail composition will vary, however, as follows materials be nailed into. Masonry nails are case-hardened, as are the special nails supplied with joist hangers and other metal connectors. Do not use reader nails to attach them.

**Other metals.** Because some metals corrode when mixed, you should match nail composition to the metal present. The choice of nails includes aluminum, stainless steel, brass, copper, and galvanized and zinc-coated.

**Exposure to the weather, corrosion.** Neither stainless steel nor aluminum nails will stain, but the former are very expensive, and the latter are brittle and somewhat tricky to nail. Galvanized nails, which are reasonably priced, will stay in only a little amount where the hammer nails chip for coating of the heat; hence, seal galvanized nails as soon as possible with a primer. Galvanize nails are also specified when framing with redwoods or treated lumber, which will corrode nails.

**Holding Power.** Nails that are resin coated, cement coated, or hot dipped galvanized hold better. Hot dips are particularly good for attaching exterior sheathing.

**Screws and Bolts.** Screws and bolts have greater holding power than nails, yet they are easily removed and reused.

**Screws.** The materials being used will dictate the choice of the screw, its composition and its shape. Softwood screws are mostly made of soft metal and are coarse-threaded; harder woods work best with screws with much finer threads. Since metal is usually thinner than wood, sheet metal screws are smaller and more self-tapping. Because screws are of soft metal, it is easy to strip their slots or twist off the heads. One trick journeyman carpenters use is to pre-drill pilot holes, especially when drilling into hardwood, using a drill bit slightly smaller than the screw diameter.

**Bolts.** Bolts are used to join major building members such as a sill plate to the foundation, as well as to join beams to steel plates, and studs to masonry. The length varies greatly. Some are huge bolts more than an inch in diameter and longer than two feet. There are several types of specialty bolts: molly toggle, spring, and gravity. The molly bolt allows attachment to thin services such as drywall; the molly stays in place even when the bolt is withdrawn. Toggle bolts and spring allow the attachment of a heavy load to a hollow wall.

## Metal Connectors

Offer wood-to-wood connections superior to most traditional methods.

## Hangers

Joist hangers are used when you want to add joist but aren't able to end nail. There are special joist hangers for single joist, double joist, and beams. Most builders are familiar with their applications.

## Straps.

Straps function primarily to keep joints from pulling apart. Perforated nailing plates, or gang plates, join the top plates of intersecting walls, as do the tee plates. There are straps intended to straddle the ridge board and tie opposing rafter pairs together; and strap connectors that keep for platforms from separating, much as shear walling dose. Twist straps, for hurricane ties, have a 90° twist to join rafters to top plates and thereby fight the tenancy of roofs to lift during a strong crosswind.

## Hold-downs.

Hold-downs are massive steel brackets that hold framing to foundations, and when used with long threaded rod called all-threads link framing on different floors. When retro-fitting to a foundation, use epoxy to attach hold-down bolts to concrete.

Post anchors and caps. Post anchors secure post to foundations. Many times they are cast in concrete, and other times red heads or concrete anchors are used to secure the post anchors. A post cap resembles a pair of U brackets, set at a right angle to each other; one U, upside down, straddles the top of the cap, while the other, right side up, receives the beam on which to joist it.

## Adhesives.

**Construction Adhesives**. A large group of adhesives is used to bond sheathing to framing members. These adhesives come in caulking tubes. Most construction adhesives are latex based and used to bridge minor irregularities, reduce squeaks, and so on. They also grip well to clean dry surfaces. Construction adhesives allow the builder to use far fewer nails. Construction adhesives vary greatly. There are specialty adhesives depending on what type of material will be used.

**Mastics.** This is a broad family of adhesives that can bond to large surface areas, such as tiles and paneling. Generous applications of the mastics fill minor imperfections in the subsurface. Mastics paste is spread with a notched trowel, other types with caulking guns. Because mastic paste is highly water resistant, it is often used to "bed" bathroom tiles.

**Epoxy.** Epoxies are available in many forms, usually two part mixtures of resin hardeners. Because the setting time is brief, press the parts together for best results. Exceptions are the cases of setting all-thread anchors or setting rebar, in which case you would first drill the holes with a rotor hammer, then use a bottle brush to thoroughly clean out the hole, and follow this up with an air compressor using an attachment to blow out the holes. Then apply a generous amount of epoxy, working the dowels back and forth in a circular motion and then up and down, working out the air pockets before allowing to set and dry.

**Acrylic.** A good glue use for outdoor use, it is quick drying, extremely strong, and completely waterproof. Work with small amounts for best results; clean up with acetone.

**Contact cement.** Commonly used to bond veneers and laminates to a base material, often particle board. Both surfaces to be attached are covered with a thin brushing of contact cement, allowed to dry, and then pressed firmly together. Once the sheets come in contact with each other, separation or realignment is all but impossible.

**Epoxy resins.** For exterior use. There are many brands, such as Water Plug and Thoroseal, which solidify on contact with water. Well-known for their strength, epoxies can bond different materials where almost nothing else will.

# CHAPTER 9

## Building Systems

One of the most common methods used to frame homes is the platform framing system. Platform framing gets its name because once the platform is finished carpenters have a smooth level surface to build off called a platform. This makes the framing of walls much easier than having to frame walls on an un-even surface.

**Carpenter Nailing Plywood to Floor Joist in Platform Framing System**

Walls are framed by bottom and top plates joined with 2 x 4, dug fir lumber called king studs. The wall may also have headers to carry the load over openings such as doors and windows to the foundation. Trimmer studs then help support the weight of the headers and cripple's short lengths of 2 x 4, or 2 x 6, lumber to support the weight of the window sill. Lay-out for studs is usually 16" OC—an acronym for "on center," in laymen's terms it is the distance in inches from the center of one stud to another. All these members depending on the plans help frame walls that are load bearing or non-load-bearing walls. Once the platform is complete carpenters lay out two 2 x 4, side by side and lay out the stud placement on the top and bottom plates by hooking a tape measure at one end of the plates and marking every 16 inches. Once these marks are complete you can come back with a Quick Square and mark an X on one side of the lay-out lines. Make sure you continue to stay on the same side of the line, either the right-hand side or the left, so you maintain your 16 in. centers for your studs. Once the wall is nailed together with a framer's nail gun that shoots 16 common nails from the top and bottom plates into the studs, then diagonal measurements can be taken to make sure the framed wall is square before 2 x 4 are nailed, called diagonal bracing, to keep the wall stiff and square before being raised by a group of men. Below is a picture of a two story building that was framed using this method.

**Two Story Building Using the Platform Framing System**

There is another system of framing walls you see little of anymore. It's called balloon framing. What is balloon framing? It's when the walls are framed using studs that run from the bottom plate to the top plate on buildings over one story. This was an earlier way of framing walls before platform framing was developed and became the standard. I won't speak on this way of framing much because, first, you hardly see this method used anymore, and second, because all of my framing experience has been with the platform framing method used most today.

One system used for building concrete walls that is fast and efficient is the tilt-up walls system. You see this method of construction used in industrial centers and business parks. Just what is a tilt-up wall and how does it get its name? These walls are made from concrete and are usually one-story buildings. The forms for the walls are constructed on the ground, making it much safer to work on than cast in place concrete walls. This also allows for faster and efficient construction. A metal embed is placed at the top of the wall, and a crane can be hooked up to this and raised up, hence the name "tilt-ups." This method is so efficient you can see the walls of business parks and industrial centers raised up within days depending on the size of the work crews.

**Wall panel forms** are used to cast in place concrete. This building system differs from Tilt-Up construction where all form work is done on the ground. Wall panels must be worked on after they have been raised up, which increases the danger and decreases the efficiency of constructing these walls. Wall panels must be buttoned up with taper ties or snap ties and kicked off with wailers and strong backs to withstand the forces and pressure of the concrete being poured. This system of construction is often used in large commercial projects like high rise buildings, bridge work and infrastructure. After the walls are poured and allowed to set up, the material used to construct these walls is stripped away and can be cleaned and used again if needed. One of the main benefits of this building system is that cast in place forms can take on any shape an architect can dream up.

**Concrete Pump Used to Deliver Concrete to Forms**

There are several building systems used to construct concrete floors or decks. One of the most popular is the **Atlas deck system**. Many deck systems have similar components and hardware that allow journeyman carpenters to erect concrete decks in a fast and efficient manner. Most systems are constructed in a grid-like pattern that is inter-locked and braced for high strength. The Atlas system's main components are the frame, the legs & feet, sleeves and adjustment saddles, and the cross braces. At the base of the frame are metal square feet. You can adjust the height by turning a lever that screw the leg up or down. Frames have round opening on the tops and bottoms that allow the frames to slide over and down the legs at the bottoms and allow saddles to slide down the opening in the frame on the top. The saddles are adjusted by a lever that screws up or down just like the legs. High decks are erected by stacking light-weight aluminum frames on top of each other. Metal pins lock the frames in place. There are locking pins that allow metal X bracing to slip over and lock the frames together. Once the frame is erected it is checked for both plumb and level to make sure the framing is strong and sturdy. Joist with nailing strip run perpendicular to the stringers. On top of the joist is nailed three-quarter inch 4 by 8 feet sheets of multi-dense overlay (MDO) plywood. This has an oil-based surface for easy stripping after the concrete has set up and the forms are ready to be stripped. This system allows for the construction of high decks. The Atlas system is used on high decks like hotel lobbies on high-rise buildings. The system being used below is similar to the Atlas system.

**Similar to the Atlas Deck Framing**

Other popular concrete deck systems in use are the **Table system, Peri system,** and the **Titan system**. First, we will discuss the table system. This is a prefabricated system of table forms. These tables are then raised by a crane in huge sections to complete the deck. The table system is pieced together like a puzzle with small gaps in between framed in to make a completed deck. Once the tables are landed on the completed concrete deck below, the legs that are pinned up underneath can be dropped, braced and set. Then all is that needed to complete the deck is the edge forms and the details such as block outs etc. The benefit of using this system is that the deck is completed in large sections, speeding up the time needed to complete a concrete deck. A good contractor will weigh the costs versus the benefits before deciding to use the table system or any other concrete deck system.

Pre-cast concrete. Pre-cast concrete can come in unlimited shapes and forms but due to the weight of concrete when transporting is many times confined to smaller firms such as K-Rail barricades you see on the freeways and pre-cast stairs for buildings.

Structural steel is another system used when building the skeleton of modern high-rise buildings. One main component of these buildings are the I-beams used in this process, which can weigh several tons. Structural steel is used in large high-rise construction projects but can also be used in smaller buildings. Buildings that are constructed this way can be erected fast. Iron and steel workers lock the steel members in place with very strong nuts and bolts before welding certain strategic parts together. The decking used in this construction is called Pan decking. It's made of metal sheets with channels incorporated in them to hold concrete. Pan decking is light and strong and an efficient way of decking buildings constructed with steel. Structural steel was first used in construction in the 19th century and has proven its strength and durability for over 100 years. Steel helped build modern city high rises after the turn of the 20th century. Steel structures have a long life spans with little or no maintenance to maintain the skeleton of the structure. Unlike wood, water rot and termites are not a problem. Most steel structures are coated with a substance called Mono-coat, which is a fire retardant, acts to increase the melting temperature of steel, and functions as a rust protector.

**Structural Steel Buildings Skeleton**

The next deck systems we will talk about are the Titan and Peri system, which are similar to one another. Each one of these is completed by a shoring system that is inter-locked in a grid-like pattern to complete the deck. Adjustable steel poles called shoring (because they shore up and support the deck) are connected by aluminum stringers and joist with the ends, having an aluminum lip that slides into a groove at the bottom of the stringers. Once the first section is built other sections can be added to complete the deck. Once the plywood is nailed into the joist the system is complete and ready for someone to check elevations with a laser. This system is fast and efficient to construct by a knowledgeable journeyman carpenter and crew. One benefit of this and similar systems is that once the deck has been poured with concrete and allowed to set up, the shoring poles have a head that drops and allows for removal of the stringers and joist while the re-shoring remains in place. Below is an example of a similar re-shoring system in place.

**Re-shoring in Place to Support Deck**

**Engineered roof trusses** are constructed off site and later delivered to the job-site for installation. They are often made from glue laminated and micro laminated materials. This process makes them extremely strong and less likely to warp and bend over time like natural lumber. Glue-lams for short are made by gluing, compressing and baking wood stacked on top of each other at very high temperatures. Engineered trusses installation, often called rolling trusses, is accomplished by having a crane or Gradall deliver them to the roof upside down in between the top plates. The two end trusses are then stood upright and nailed in with vertical 2 x 4 stiffeners. A string line can be pulled in between both trusses to act as a guide to help center the remaining trusses once they are rolled up in an upright position, then space blocking can be installed to establish centers of trusses and to form the ridge line for the roof. This method of framing a roof can be fast and efficient. Once the trusses have been raised and nailed into the walls top plate, then plywood can be nailed in a staggered pattern to help stiffen the trusses. In the picture below you can see trusses delivered to a job-site with a small crane to aid in delivery to the residential building for installation. Two journeyman carpenters can install the roof trusses.

**Roof Trusses Delivered to Residential Job-site**

# CHAPTER 10

## Trade Specializations

Carpentry and the construction trades have many specialties you can branch out into. Once you become a journeyman carpenter you may specialize in one area of carpentry or you may go into a whole other trade. The basics you learn as a carpenter apprentice apply to all parts of construction, so you can have a jump start if you try another career in construction. First, I would like to talk about form carpenters, or sometimes referred to as **form setters.** This carpenter's responsibilities and skills center on building and setting forms to hold concrete. Even as a form setter there are many sections of specialization you can branch out to or focus on. Examples are bridge carpenters that work on the freeway and road systems' infrastructure. Then you have carpenters who work on water treatment plants, underground projects, dams, and parking structures. I am sure there are other specialties like curb and gutter form carpenters I have forgotten to mention. The point I am getting at is that any one of these sections can become a specialty in your role as a form setter.

The specialty you end up following is a choice limited only by your imagination and willingness. My recommendation to help your career excel and to have the best chance of staying employable is to gain experience in several sections before specializing in one. This way if work ever becomes slow in one, or if an opportunity should present itself in another field, you will capitalize on it by having experience in a broad range of form setting. Then later you can always seek and find a specialization you enjoy or are drawn too. The benefit of staying with and developing a specialized skill in one area is that you can often receive a higher rate of pay than someone who is not specializing in any one capacity. Once you know the inside and out of a certain part of construction you can run work and have a much better chance of moving up your career field in that specialty subject and training. Form setting like other areas of construction takes hard work, dedication and a willingness to learn new techniques and methods to remain at the top of your game and to remain competitive. Form setting can also be rewarding both financially and emotionally. Riding over a bridge you help construct or visiting a finished building with the family once it is complete and knowing you played a part in its completion is a gratifying feeling as is standing on a high-rise deck looking out at the sun rise in the morning and knowing that your skill as a carpenter has made that building possible. Oh! what these eyes have seen. Being a carpenter has let me see some of the greatest structures built that will still stand after I'm gone and help benefit the next generation.

**Concrete Form Work for Building Step Footings**

**Wood framers** are carpenters who specialize in building and framing wood structures such as apartment complexes and residential tracts. Housing tracts are sections of developments in which builders construct new housing projects. They have several different designs at several price points for home buyers. Framing carpenters are the ones who build these tracts for the contractor on these housing projects. Some framers specialize in building custom million dollar homes in exclusive gated communities. They are skilled at their trade and work around expensive materials and finishes in custom homes. Compared to form setting carpenters they don't have to carry as many tools in their bags and as much safety equipment. Their work is not as physically demanding as concrete form setters. Framers also have a more relaxed working environment than form carpenters and are often allowed to wear short pants and listen to music while working. Because of the fewer hazards, less physically demanding work and less restrictions, framing often pays less than concrete form work. Some framers who have been in the field for years and run work may earn as much as form setter carpenters. Most of the rank-and-file carpenters earn less than form setters. Some framers specialize in metal stud framing. This framing is used in commercial construction. There are many similarities between wood and metal stud framing. The basics like lay-out on-center and framing members are the same, the main difference is in the materials used to frame. In metal stud framing the studs are installed in the top and bottom channels and screwed in from the side with self-tapping screws. One benefit of metal studs is that they are much lighter than wood. Metal studs when constructed right have a much longer life span than wood, due mostly to termite concerns or moisture problems. The tools used for metal framing are a chop saw with a metal blade and a screw gun. Self-tapping screws are used instead of nails and metal channels are used instead of wood blocking. One hazard of working with metal studs are the sharp edges on the material and the ones that can be created by cutting the material with a chop saw or tin snips.

Almost all poured concrete needs to be finished to function as an end product. **Concrete finishers** finish concrete to a smooth finish. Finishers have special tools to work with to help them accomplish this. Their primary tools are a bull float, Fresno, margin trowel and other specialty tools. Some finishers can build and set concrete forms, which allows the greatest chance of remaining used during boom and slow times in the construction trade. There are also many finishes for concrete, such as different colors, stamps and patterns that can be used on concrete. Finishers can provide the needed finish that designers and architects call for on the building plans. Like any other trade there are many specialties as a finisher. Stamped and colored concrete is one area of specialization. It may take many years of training and hands-on experience to learn how to finish concrete. Something else to consider in finishing concrete is that it can be hard on the body. Many finishers and form setters end up with joint and back pain later in life due to the physical demand placed on the body after years in the trade.

**Cabinet installers** are needed both in commercial and residential construction projects. This is another spin-off of carpentry. Some carpenters specialize in this one area of construction. They manage lay-out and installation of cabinets and countertops. Cabinets and countertops go hand in hand. Cabinet and countertop installers work with expensive finished materials and one must be extra careful when working with these materials not to damage or break these products. Fine and exotic wood such as walnut, spruce, elm, and cherry woods are often used in fine cabinet work. Materials for countertops can be marble, granite, slate and wood laminates. Precise and exact measurements must be taken when laying out and cutting finished materials such as cabinets and countertops. Finish work often requires special tools to help cabinet & counter top installers perform their work. Working conditions are pleasant. Cabinet and countertop installers can be used in housing tracts, fine homes, commercial building, schools, government buildings and research and development laboratories. If you enjoy doing fine detailed work inside and out of the sun this may be a specialty to enter. I recommend taking free classes in cabinet making and installation at the Home Depot or at your local ROP campus to gain basics training if this interests you.

*Floor Installations* is another area of carpentry specialization to consider. Carpenters who work with flooring materials and do installations of hardwood floors, floor laminates, clay floor tiles, and marble flooring. Working conditions are very similar to cabinet and countertop installers. Working is usually indoors out of the sun around finish materials and surfaces. Floor installation often requires a set of tools unique to this trade. Care must be taken not to break and damage finish materials and surfaces. Quality work is a high priority in this area of specialization just like any other area of carpentry. Long hours of working on your knees may be required. Free classes are offered if you wish to learn more about this area of specialization.

*Dry Wall Hangers* complete the finish wall material in buildings. They accomplish this by hanging 4 x 8 or 4 x 16 sheets of drywall in the interior of buildings. Sheets are held up the thickness of the flooring material for the bottom course. Sheet butt lines end on wall studs. Each additional course is laid out so the butt lines are staggered on the wall studs for shear strength. Sheets come in different thicknesses and are fire rated to prevent fire from traveling through walls. Heavy lifting is often requiring while sheets are hung. Screws or nails are used to hang the sheets and secure them to wall studs.

**Mud and tape workers** finish the butt joints left by dry wall hangers. Many also do wall textures. Their main tools are a mud pan, plus an assortment of drywall knives that come in different sizes and widths. Many learn to walk on stilts to help them reach higher areas that need to be mud and taped. Mud and tapers also use joint tape on top of drywall mud compound and over butt joints to cover and help conceal the seams that drywall sheets create. The dry wall mud compounds I'm referring to above come in dry and premixed forms. Drywall mud when ready for use has a rich smooth creamy texture that spreads easily. These guys are experts in covering seams and butt joints. The end product is one smooth seamless wall. Mud & tape guys usually also do wall textures. Wall & ceiling textures are created by a machine called a hopper that sprays joint compound through a nozzle in various concentrations and thicknesses on walls and ceilings. Then depending on the texture a special tool called a knock down knife is used to knock down the dry wall compound into a specific wall texture. Some tradesmen specialize in stucco. This is a thin coating of concrete and mortar like material applied as a finish material on the exterior of buildings. Underneath the coating of stucco is applied a weather proofing paper and chicken coop wiring to help the stucco bond with the exterior surface. Coloring can be added to stucco in dye mixed in with the stucco. Stucco is applied in a three-step process called the brown coat, the scratch coat, and the finish coat. Special trowels are used for the stucco application process.

**Insulation** is a material applied between the studs in walls and in between the roof joist to help retain heat used to warm homes and buildings. Insulation comes with an R-rating that applies to heat value retaining qualities. Older insulation in buildings can be a health hazard to remove. Breathing protection, eye protection and gloves should always be used when removing older insulation that may become airborne. The material used to make most insulation is fiber glass based. Breathing this material into your lungs can carry serious and life-threatening hazards if proper protective safety equipment is not used during installation and removal. Properly rated and installed insulation can help cut heating and energy cost and provide great savings to building owners and occupants.

Another trade specialization is **roof carpenters**. Roofers repair and install new roofing materials and systems. A roofing system is all the materials and products needed to build and maintain the roof, such as framing members that are needed, the plywood, roofing paper, roof shingles, nails and tar. Roofers often work high off the ground in direct sun. Sometime roof repair or new installation may require a weather proofing hot mop. This is accomplished by heating roofing tar to hundreds of degrees and having roofers mop the roof with hot tar to help weather proof the structure. This can be very unpleasant work with the potential of severe burns if one is not extremely careful.

**Glazers** install commercial windows in high-rise buildings. People entering this field should not be afraid of working at extreme heights. **Doors installation and hardware** is yet another area of specialization. Carpenters who enter this field should be good at figuring out mechanical hardware installation and be able to follow templates and diagrams when needed to install hardware. Door installation may require extended periods of heavy lifting depending on the door size and locations of the installations. Special carts and dollies are often used to help transport doors to installation points. Being able to read building plans and door schedules for installation will be of great benefit in gaining work and advancing career opportunities in this field. Special tools are often required in this field. An individual able to follow directions and work with basic and sometimes complex forms of hardware is a plus when entering this field. Doors come in many shapes and sizes and some carpenters may specialize in residential or commercial door installations. Remaining fast, efficient and able to do a quality job is very important just like other trades of construction.

**Plumbers** are tradesmen who run the pipes that deliver drinking water and get rid of waste in modern structures. Just like carpenters and electricians, journeyman plumbers earn a good working wage. They have their own union and apprenticeship programs. Journeyman plumbers can specialize in residential or commercial plumbing. Sometimes digging may be required to install their pipe delivery and waste systems. Many plumbers learn, and are sometimes certified, to operate digging equipment to aid them in the installation of these systems.

**Electricians** bring wiring and power sources to buildings. What would our modern way of life be like if not for the power of electricity? Electricians are the tradesmen paid to bring this power safely into our homes and structures. We rely on this power for our comfort, entertainment, safety, and convenience in almost all areas in our lives. This trade pays good wages and has plenty of opportunities to advance for black people interested in entering this field. Electricians just like carpenters have their own union and apprenticeship training for people who want to learn more or enter this construction trade. I know of a black man name Carl who has been in this trade for over 20 years and owns his own successful company. Electricity like any other power must be respected or it could cause injury or death. It can however be safe to work with if you understand the science and basic principles that govern this power and work safely around it. Many younger black men and women are needed to enter this trade and take advantage of the economic opportunities this field of construction offers. For more information, contact your local Black Contractors Association on the qualifications and opportunities to enter this field.

**Electrician Pulling Flex Conduit for Electrical Systems on Commercial Concrete Deck Form.**

# CHAPTER 11

## Applying at Job-Sites

What do I look for? Finding and keeping a job is what it's all about. That is true in the general job market and it is no different in the construction industry. The term I like to use in finding work is to be a "go-getter." What does it mean? Well, you may not find it in *Webster's Dictionary* or in a Google Search. Here is my definition for the sake of this chapter: a go-getter is someone looking for a job that does not wait for the phone to ring for employment. They are out there beating the pavement finding employment opportunities. Companies are always hiring. Do you know what signs to look for?

**Job-site That's Seeking to Hire Carpenters**

I like to plan my job search on Sunday before the week starts. Having a plan lets you hit the ground running Monday morning instead of wasting valuable time that could be better used in your job search. Saturday and Sunday are great days you can use to get ready for your employment search throughout the coming week. Watch for construction cranes and job-site activity as you travel about during the week. Write detailed notes and take pictures about what stage the project is in, such as whether the contractor is just excavating, grading and digging footings. This means the job-site will not be manning up, which is construction talk for hiring carpenters, for about two to three months. It takes the contractor at least that long to bring in the job-site trailers, and install the lagging for retaining walls, around the job-site perimeter, and temp power. I rarely waste my time applying to projects in the grading and excavation phase.

**Job-site Performing Grading Work and Probably
Too Early to Apply for Work**

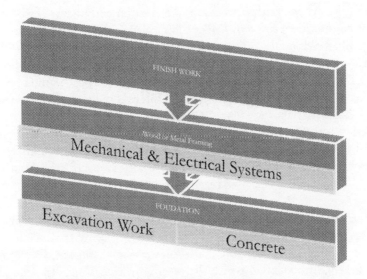

**Stages of Construction to Complete a Building**

Before I get ahead of myself I like to break down a construction project in stages. Stage one is job-site excavation. That is what we went over in the above paragraph. That include everything to get the project ramped up. Stage two I will title pouring or building the foundation. This is an ideal time to apply for work. This stage is when you will scan for concrete forms for slab on grade work and column forms. One note, this is the foundation on the West Coast in North America. On the East Coast there may be pier footings or elevated footings on block walls. Another difference is that on the East Coast you may see storm cellars in residential construction. The thing to focus on regardless of what part of the country you live in is foundation work. If you can get hired at this stage, there is the greatest chance of long-term employment. Most general contractors will bring in employees from other job-sites before hiring outside their organization, so learn to expect this. When the foundation stage is in progress things pick up in manpower and construction activities.

## The Early Bird Gets the Worm

I like to compare the construction trade to the armed services, because we get more done by 9:00 am than most people do during the day. That being said, construction days start early. Depending on what's being done, a day could start as early as 3:00 am. Are you an early riser? If not, this may not be the career for you. I, like most construction workers, wake up about 4:30 am Monday - Friday. Have you ever heard of the saying "The early bird gets the worm"? This is true in construction. When I'm seeking work I have usually stopped by four different job-sites by 8:00 am. The real challenge is deciding what one should be visited first. During my morning search I can only be at one place at a time, which contradicts the rule of meeting with the foreman before the workday begins. As an illustration: if four different job-sites start at 7:00 am, you can't see all the different foreman before the work day. This is when priorities must be set as to which site you visit has the greatest chance of being hired.

Construction work days are mostly between the hours of 7:00 am and 3:30 pm. If the workday starts at 7:00 am, make sure you arrive to talk with the foreman about employment no later than 6:30 am. Remember that the early bird gets the worm; the reason for this is once the workday starts you won't get his full attention. Most of the time I will ask other workers on the job-site what the foreman's name is and what does he look like before I knock on the job trailer door and introduce myself. After my introduction I go into the two-minute commercial I will explain later. It is my job experience, trainings, and personal traits and why I should be hired presented within two minutes. I found out through experience that two minutes is about how much time you need to spark interest without overstaying your welcome. In this field the early mornings will be the most productive times and present the greatest opportunities of finding employment. I have learned to embrace the early mornings and look forward to the sunrise because I know this is when things happen for me. So do yourself a favor and set the coffee pot and alarm the night before and be headed out the door no later than 5:00 am, and you will give yourself the greatest chance of finding employment.

## Getting Past Gatekeepers

One obstacle you will face during your job search are the gatekeepers. This refers to any person who stands in your way of talking with whoever is hiring at that job-site, such as security, company personnel and employees etc. This is when some determination and creativity is called for. The following are just two recollections of times I needed to get past gatekeepers to gain employment. I remember one job-site where the security measures were tight and a security guard was at a guard post stopping visitors. I had already done my research and knew who the general contractor performing the work was. When I was asked what the purpose of my visit was, I said that I was an employee of the contractor and was allowed access. I'm not recommending that you do this; I'm stating that sometimes you must do whatever is necessary to gain access to who is hiring. On another occasion I was walking up to the job trailer when an employee of the contractor informed me they were not hiring at the job-site. After they had walked away I walked in the trailer, asked if I could have a moment with the superintendent and went into my two-minute commercial. I received a call from the contractor a few days later telling me I was hired and to report to work at the beginning of the work week. The lesson to be learned is that the only person whose opinion should matter to you is the person who has the authority to hire. That person is the foreman. Don't let gatekeepers deter you from your mission of finding employment. On that note, sometimes gatekeepers can be a valuable source of information. Be polite and get as much information about the company as you can. Also ask what's going on at the job-site and if they are hiring, and don't forget to ask for the foreman's contact information and what is the best time to catch him. I even inquired on occasions what type of vehicle they drove so I would know when they were on site.

## Two Minutes and Counting

Job-sites are busy places. The job trailer is the nerve center for all the planning that is done for all the construction activities. Superintendents and job foreman are busy people. They are often having meetings during the workday with building inspectors, engineers and other tradesmen just to name a few. So the first thing you need to remember when walking in a job trailer is to respect their time. There is nothing more likely to ruin your chance of employment than not remembering to respect their time. I developed a mental stopwatch that is set the moment I enter their space. I have learned from experience you're permitted about two minutes to explain why you are there and what your qualifications are, and why you are the best person for the carpenter position. That's a lot to cover in two minutes. So you must be straight to the point and not waste any time. Plus, all this must be done while projecting confidence in yourself and your abilities.

Let none of this overwhelm you or frighten you. I have undergone this countless times and so can you. In real estate they use the phrase "Location,

location, location." In the two minutes and counting scenario we substitute that for "Practice, practice, practice." I have done this so many times I can do my two-minute pitch or commercial in my sleep. You must master your pitch as well to stay employed. Right now I will walk you through what I say from the knock and entering point at the job trailer. Here we go; Knock knock! "My name is Desmond; may I speak with the job-site foreman please?" If I am lucky enough to catch him he would respond with, "How can I help you?" Looking him straight in the eye, I say, "I'm a journeyman carpenter, I have been in the trade for 15 plus years. My specialty is setting forms for concrete. I possess working experience with the Atlas, Peri and Titan deck systems. I was lead carpenter for Morley Builders on the deck crew and could cut the time to completing a deck from five to three days. I see you are getting ready to pour the slab on grade today. Are you looking to hire a good carpenter? I would like to be a part of the team." That's it!

Your two-minute commercial will differ from mine depending on your experience. I recommend spending a full day getting yours together and perfecting giving the presentation to a friend or significant other until it is flawless and you can give it on demand with no thought... This will be one of your most effective tools when talking to superintendents and foreman when seeking work.

## The Elevator Pitch

From this moment forward when I refer to the elevator pitch its meaning will be the same as your two-minute commercial. So what is an *elevator pitch*? It's the time you possess when you are traveling between floors in an elevator, by capitalizing on the opportunity to introduce yourself and your product or services to someone you meet on the elevator. Keep in mind that you will have less than two minutes to accomplish this task. This is a great way to build a business, network or apply for a job at a construction site. What will be the content of your elevator pitch if you haven't been in the trade and hold little experience? Remember earlier I recommended spending a full day getting material together and practicing this pitch until perfected. You can include any construction related work you experienced, paid for or not. I recommend talking to a career counselor and enrolling in an interview readiness class. In San Diego we have Career Metro Centers in all different areas of the county where you can take free classes that will help you prepare for your elevator pitch. I have taken these classes numerous times and organized all materials in a special folder I can refer to if I'm looking to change or perfect mine. Also on that note I recommend spending a day getting your resume together. Going through the exercise of getting a polished resume together will force you to look long and hard at your prior job experience. Even though resumes are rarely used when applying for work at job-sites you should keep yours up-dated and ready if ever called for. I have landed previous jobs by just sending my resume and getting the interview. A resume is just one more tool to use and have ready during your job search. Think of it this way: carpenters must use a variety of tools to accomplish different jobs. In your job search you need a wide range of tools to call on to accomplish finding employment at job-sites.

Now that you have all the material to complete your elevator pitch, it's time to practice it until it's memorized and flawless. Find a friend or partner and explain what you are trying to do and how important this exercise is, then practice until your elevator pitch is flawless.

## Using the Language of the Trade

Did you realize that construction has a language of its own? When carpenters talk among themselves they use the terms and lingo used in the construction industry. Are you familiar with common terms used out at the construction site daily? As a professional tradesman you are expected to not only understand these terms but also to communicate effectively with other craftsmen who use the lingo of construction. The reason this is so important is because when you apply for work at a job-site, using these terms is a powerful way you can use to let foreman appreciate that you have been working in the trade, and have the knowledge of what terms are used in the industry. Form carpenters often refer to strong backs, whalers and taper ties when building wall forms for concrete. Framers in residential construction often refer to king studs, cripples and rafters when building tracts of homes. Finish carpenters refer to miter cuts, beveled edges and curfs for the precision cuts. Whatever your field of specialization of construction is, do yourself a big favor and learn the language.

Like in any other industry it takes years to learn the language, but the payoff is tremendous. One of the first things I was taught as a carpenter apprentice was to learn and memorize the different grades and selections of wood. They have different plywood you would use in building depending on the project. Specialized plywood for building forms for concrete such as MDO that is an oil-based product that has a smooth fine surface for easy stripping after concrete has set up. Another is rated plywood for building shear walls—the list is extensive. The point is, if you want to perform at the top of your game out in the field you need to know what wood or material is called for according to what type of construction and purpose. They developed many resources to learn this information that is free or low cost. I suggest you build yourself a reference library of books and information you can study and refer to as needed. The internet is also another place you can gather a wealth of information to increase your knowledge of the terms and different materials they have and continue to develop. YouTube also has hundreds of videos to increase your knowledge in every area you could ever imagine for construction projects and the lingo or language associated with that project. So there you have it: there are no excuses any more in the information age to increase your understanding and vocabulary on any subject.

## Looking the Part

The next couple of paragraphs will touch on the subject of looking the part when applying for work at construction job-sites. Every area of industry and profession has a dress code. Just as a lawyer wouldn't show up in court at a case wearing dirty pants, we in the construction field require a dress code we adhere to. Just what does a carpenter dress like? Let's start with the basic requirements to enter any job-site. This may seem like a waste of time to go over to many people who have been in the field for any length of time. However, it still amazes me to see how many people will walk on a job-site and not have the basic dress requirements needed not only to enter the site but to be considered for employment. For one, you will need an OSHA approved hard hat, safety vest, boots and safety glasses while on site at all times. The newest trend is gloves as well on many union sites.

When applying for work on construction job-sites make sure you wear all your basic PPEs. This will put your best foot forward and let the employer know you take safety seriously and are ready to work. Some other basic requirements that many people overlook or forget when applying for work is long pants and no jewelry. If you possess a nice watch or ring do yourself a favor and leave these items at home or in your car before entering a job-site. I recommend purchasing some rugged durable pants to wear like carpenter jeans, Dickie's or Levi's 501. Shirts may be worn on some sites without a safety vest if the colors are a bright orange or florescent green with stripes that illuminate. Many carpenters wear two shirts, one long and one short sleeve. This combination helps to regulate the body's heat on hot days. During cold mornings this helps to keep the heat insulated by your body to help keep you warm. During summer months the short-sleeve shirt can be taken off to help cool yourself down or kept on by itself in hot weather. Many carpenters also wear head bandanas to help regulate the heat that is generated or escapes for your head during the work day. When it is cold this helps to keep your head warm and trap heat from leaving. During summer months or in extremely hot weather the bandana can be wet with room temperature water to help cool down your head in a hurry or sometimes just removed... These tips will help you appear the part of a professional and send a message that you have been in the trade and are familiar with the basic dress code.

## Wear your carpenter bags when applying at jobsites

When you are seeking employment at construction sites always wear your carpenter bags. This ties into a principle and strategy that we earlier talked about on making a good first impression. Job superintendents and foreman are looking for people that are ready to work. Always be prepared to start working on the spot if hired. This means having on your carpenter bags and tools and bringing your lunch box when applying for work. This also sends a subconscious message to the employer that you are a serious person for employment consideration. You will also separate yourself from the pack of unprepared tradesmen seeking work.

## Making Eye Contact

When applying for work at job-sites and talking to the foreman always look them in the eye when speaking. Have you ever noticed that when someone is talking to you and not making eye contact we feel like they are either not paying attention, trying to hide something, or not confident in themselves or their abilities? None of the above is a good thing during a job interview. Whenever I am speaking to foreman or superintendents about employment I make myself a mental note to keep eye contact when speaking. One, I want them to remember my face so if I return at a later date to re-apply they remember me. Two, I want them to see I am a confident professional with nothing to hide and feel myself worthy of the position. You would be surprised how many people do not make eye contact today while speaking. You should strive to do this whenever talking to others. It is a great habit to develop better communication skills. Three, I want to gather as much information as possible about the project so I can write good notes and use all information to help me land the job.

## A Firm Handshake

When applying for work at a job-site and talking to the foreman or superintendent face to face make sure you give a firm handshake. This is so basic that its importance is often overlooked. First impressions often decide if you will get hired on the spot or remembered and called for employment at a later date. A firm handshake can send a sub-conscious message to others letting them know that you are confident. If your handshake is meek and flimsy, it might mean you lack self-confidence and don't hold a high value of yourself as a person. Here is something I would like to share with you: others see what you see in yourself. If you place a high value on yourself and abilities, others will. On the flip side, you don't want to crush the other person's hand either; this could be viewed as being disrespectful and trying to dominate the other person. So make yourself a mental note: always make eye contact and give a firm handshake.

## Being Persistent

Many times in life and applying for work in takes persistence to get what we desire. Timing is everything when trying to get hired. Many jobs I possessed in the past was because I would not give up and continued to stop by weekly to show my interest in getting hired. I recall one time when I was out of work a company by the name of JR Concrete had a job in Escondido CA. I showed up weekly before the superintendent would arrive. When he arrived at about 6:00 am in the morning I would without him asking help him unload his truck. This continued for about a month when one morning he turned and, "Said get your bags, I'm hiring you." Sometimes you must exhibit how much you want to work. Many times when applying to a job-site when the workers are doing their morning stretches as a group I will join in and even stay for the morning safety meeting. My goal at this point is to be seen as one of the team. I believe it's hard to see someone week after week showing up and even stretching with the men and attending safety meetings without giving him a shot to prove himself as a worker. Men respect persistence. Wouldn't you feel obligated to do the same if you were doing the hiring?

With that being said, it can be hard and frustrating to stay consistent when applying to job-sites. Sometimes it pays off and sometimes it doesn't. You must come to terms with this early and learn to accept this. Many times I endured showing up with promises of being hired and it did not happen. Was I angry? Yes! But the point I'm trying to make is you can't let this stop you. Nothing can stop a man that is goal driven and full of determination and purpose. You must learn to keep your spirits up and require hope to continue to go on day after day. Sometimes you endure to hear a lot of no's before you will hear a yes. Being persistent will always pay off, this is my sincere belief. Now that you possess all the tools and inside knowledge on what works and doesn't work when applying for work at job-sites, now the real work begins. You must put these things I taught you into practice, and last but not least have hope and believe in yourself and your abilities to find a job and make construction your career.

## How to Write Good Notes

We live in the information age. Getting the right leads and contacts could mean the difference between getting a job or not. When I first started out in construction and was applying to different job-sites, I did not think taking good notes was all that important. Almost twenty years later and after having applied to countless job-sites my views changed. Often when returning to a job-site I could not remember the superintendent's or foreman's name. Many times I couldn't even remember the company's name or the contact person. This would create frustration. How could I ask to speak with someone if I didn't know their name? There is also a lot of other relevant information you should take notes on when applying to job-sites. I like to write what stage the project is in and when they believe they will hire carpenters so I don't end up wasting time and gas money. Your time should be focused on applying to job-sites ready to hire. I suggest using a phone app or camera to take plenty of pictures of the work in progress. When reviewing my notes, I often refer to these pictures to remind me what stage the job is in, what's going on and when is a good date to re-apply. People also like when you remember their names. When you ask to talk to a superintendent or foreman using their name will make them think you probably know them or crossed their path before. This will give you an edge over your competition when applying for work. You also want to write a note about if they know any other job-sites you can apply to. If I don't take pen and paper I often use a voice recording phone app to record notes as soon as I leave the site while sitting in my truck so I forget nothing, then as soon as I get home I transfer it to my Microsoft Outlook calendar for follow-ups at a later date. So there you hold all the note taking strategies and secrets I use to give me an edge over the competition.

## How Laborers Can Help You Learn

Laborers can often be an invaluable source of learning for construction. The have many important roles in the completion of a building and construction project. Their main responsibilities when it come to commercial construction is stripping and organizing materials.

## Following Up after a Site Visit

Taking good notes will allow a thoughtful, productive follow-up. Many times when applying at a job-site you will not be hired on the spot and will need to follow up at a later date. This is the best time to refer back to your notes to plan the best strategy for getting back with the employer. The notes I take let me know when the best time to visit the site again is, where the job-site is located, what if any job-site security and barricades I must go through and who is the contact person. When I have this information in hand, this gives me the greatest chance when re-applying for the position. This saves me both time and money and allows me to concentrate my energy on the best prospects. I believe in personal visits over letters or phone calls. I like the benefit of looking my potential employer in the face when presenting my worth and abilities. Also, I believe it's harder to look a man in the eyes and deny him employment after several visits, than it is to do so over the phone. I walk in and say, "My name is Desmond I'm a journeyman carpenter. I stopped by a few weeks ago to speak with you. I'm still very interested in working with you and am wondering if you are ready to put on a good man like myself today." I either hear, "Okay, you're hired" or "Check back with me." Then I thank them for their time. Good follow-up strategy is how I get hired 95% of the time.

## It Isn't Over till I Win!

I'm borrowing this saying from who I consider one of the best motivational speakers I have ever heard, Les Brown. I highly recommend checking out some of his speeches on YouTube. He goes in to how you should let nothing stop you from accomplishing your dreams. It's true. Develop the mindset that you will become a success and land the job of your dreams. This is the attitude that will carry you through day in and day out when you feel like giving up on yourself and your dreams. I remember when I was a carpenter apprentice many people told me I could never become a carpenter. I even doubted myself on occasions, but had a burning desire deep in my heart to prove to myself that I would not only become a carpenter but one of the best and respected carpenters in the field. Now that's a reality, the road to success is never easy, but the journey was well worth the struggle. Now I'm leaving a legacy to my two sons Marcus and Malcolm and am living proof you can accomplish your dream of becoming a carpenter and earning good money and any dream your heart desires. Also, when things get tough and I guarantee you they will, tell yourself, "It isn't over till I win."

# CHAPTER 12

## Traveling for Work

### How Far Should You Travel

Working in construction often requires traveling to job-sites. Unlike other occupations where you might work at the same job location for many years, construction work often requires finding and locating work in different locations. Sometimes when looking for work you can find a job-site close to your house, other times it may be in another city or another state. Making good money in the construction trade often require sacrifice. This can mean working a way from loved ones for extended periods of time to work. This can put a strain on relationships by making it hard to attend football and baseball practices and school events for young children in school. You need to be asking yourself, "How far would I be willing to travel to find employment?" This is something many construction workers have to come to terms with, and I believe something that should be discussed with spouses and loved ones before a decision is made. How far would you be willing to travel to buy a house, to provide your family with medical insurance, and be able to provide a good living for your family? I have worked with many carpenters that have traveled from other states to find work and good paying jobs. I myself had traveled 6 hours to job-sites where I had to stay the week in a motel to work. It all comes down to what you and your family will sacrifice in order for you to remain employed. I weigh the pros against the cons of traveling. Some of the questions I might ask myself are: What is the potential of me working long term for this company? What are the chances of me advancing my career with this company? How much of my traveling expenses are they willing to pay? What am I trying to achieve financially at this time in my life? I might be trying to purchase a home. Am I trying to get out of debt? What other options and opportunities are available if I don't travel and take advantage of the job being offered?

## What are the Benefits of Traveling out of Town?

There's a lot that can be said about traveling to work. If you enjoy traveling, seeing new sights, locations and getting paid while doing it, then traveling out of town to work may be just the thing for you. When I was a young apprentice I had done little traveling yet so the thought of traveling to new cities was exciting. The anticipation of the road trip, staying in a motel, and seeing something new was thrilling. I had the opportunity to work on many projects out of town both large and small. I've seen many things I would never have gotten the opportunity to see had it not been for my willingness to work out of town. Soltec Pacific, a contractor where I completed my apprenticeship back in the mid-1990s had many large work contracts with colleges, military bases and schools. I got to work on the University of Irvine, University of LA, University of San Diego, and many other schools I do not recall the names of. This expanded my mind, my thinking, and my world. When I was in my teens I grew up in the San Diego area on 40th Street and joined a gang in a high crime area. Then, I thought that was the whole world. Traveling to work opened my world and let me see the possibilities open to me. Journeying also gave me the opportunity to form many personal and close relationships with other carpenters and tradesmen both here in the city of San Diego and out of town that would not have happened if it had not been for my willingness to travel. Even years later I recall memories and fun times shared out of town with carpenters and tradesmen I traveled out of town with that I remain in contact with today. This shared experience has built a closer bond of friendship between me and other tradesmen. Some of these relationships and contacts themselves have led to employment prospects. I also gained the opportunity to work on many military installations and bases. Some of them were the naval amphibious base in Coronado, California, Camp Pendleton, the naval base, and North Island. These experiences and sights were priceless and well worth the travel. One important benefit I did not mention is that companies keep employees willing to do whatever it takes to stay employed. Companies like these are looking for employees willing to travel to the project locations. These employees are often remembered and rewarded for their sacrifices through promotions, long-term employment, and other company perks not offered to the other employees who are less ready to travel. These are both tangible and intangible benefits you receive by the willingness to travel.

## What are the hassles of traveling out of town for work?

Traveling out of town can be tough. Let's face it: most people would like to work in town where after the day's work they can come home to their comfortable house and loving family. I recall the stress that leaving town would cost me when I was a young apprentice working for Soltek Pacific. Many times I suffered to wake up and be on the road at 2:00am so I could be ready to work first thing in the morning. The day before I would pack my suitcases, looking at maps and trying to locate the hotel. Plus, all the other things that go along with traveling. Another big concern of mine when traveling out of town was my vehicle breaking down. I recall this happening frequently. I remember one night when traveling to a job in Riverside California. From San Diego my truck broke down at the vehicle checkpoint in Temecula, California. This is something you don't want to happen. Not only because it is the middle of the night when taking your truck to a repair station is an impossibility, but I was also backing up traffic and vehicles at the Riverside checkpoint, which was another added stress.

My son was a newborn and my first wife had to drive up from San Diego to Marietta to drive me home, and we arranged that the vehicle be towed. Your car breaking down is a very real possibility when traveling out of town. I soon learned from experience it was best to have AAA auto insurance. Then, at least I had the peace of mind of knowing that if my vehicle broke down they would send someone to help me out with roadside help and tow my vehicle home if necessary. This helped relieve a lot of stress in a bad situation. Other challenges when traveling were taking the wrong freeway turnoff are completely getting lost. Back in the 1990s when I did most of my traveling out of town to work we had to use a Thomas Guide, which can be quite a challenge at night. Things have gotten much easier now days: having a GPS is common and most people have the GPS application on their phone that can help them out when traveling. One of the things I didn't like about traveling out of town was the long drive home on Fridays. Traffic is bad enough already when you're in town on a Friday. Try driving home during rush hour traffic out of town in a major city like LA on the

405 freeway and trying to make the drive home to San Diego. This can be a nightmare. This was often what I had to deal with when driving home.

## Traveling Allowance

Many companies give you a travel allowance when working out of town. Many times it differs from company to company. Most cover hotel expenses; some give a gas mileage expense; each company has its own policy for traveling allowances. Smaller companies want you to pay for the hotel for the week and tell you to save the receipts and they will reimburse you. Then others like Soltec Pacific, a larger company I was employed with when working out of town, already have the room paid for when you arrive for work. I myself don't like the first option of paying for the room out of my pocket and waiting to be reimbursed. I found through experience that most companies are like people: some can be trusted and others can't. The ones that promise they'll reimburse you for the hotel room can sometimes make it difficult to collect the money that's due you. When it comes to being reimbursed for your gas when traveling I've been told many times to keep track of my mileage and gas receipts when the company had no intention of ever paying me for gas. My advice is to be careful about how much money you pay out of pocket or up-front before agreeing with a company that wants you to travel.

They should foot the bill for you when traveling out of town paying for basic things like your hotel and gas. This is a personal decision you must make; only you can decide. Ask yourself what you're willing to go through or pay up-front to find employment or travel out of town. Rarely do you get paid for food expense this is something you must be prepared to pay out of your pocket.

What to Do after Work for Entertainment

After working hours when working out of town you can often be lonely and bored, especially if you're married and away from family. When I was working for Soltek Pacific and working out of town I would often come up with inexpensive ways of entertaining myself. Bear in mind I was a lot younger then and was still drinking. Soltek Pacific often sent several employees out of town to the same job-site. Sharing a room with someone else often helps with the loneliness and being bored. We often traveled in groups and would require many rooms on one floor. There were a lot of rooms visiting among each other. We also did a lot of drinking. Many of the guys would like to get together and go to strip bars and clubs, not something I recommend when you need to get up early for the next morning to go to work. One of my favorite things to do when working out of town was to see all the new sites that the city offered. New places like taco shops, movie theaters, shopping centers and parks. Eating out of town can become expensive if you don't watch your money. I often would pack sandwiches and other snacks and drinks to consume it the hotel to help cut down on expenses. They had a small refrigerator in our rooms. Other things to consider to keep you from becoming bored is watching a movie, playing a game of chess or driving around town. Some nights comprised going out for a long walk. This was a cheap way of relieving boredom and seeing new sites. A word of caution: be careful what neighborhoods you are traveling in when out of town; you could end up a victim of being crime, or even worse if you're not careful. Just use common sense when traveling in an unfamiliar city.

How You Should Prepare for the Drive Home

I recommend that you get a good night's sleep before the drive. There have been many times I underestimated the consequences of not having enough sleep and the effect it can have on your driving abilities. When I was younger, I thought I was invincible. The group of workers I traveled with would often stay up late night drinking before working the eight-hour shift and then facing the long drive home through traffic on a Friday. Sometimes the commute would be between four to six hours. Many times and several occasions when traveling out of town, on the push back home I have nearly fallen asleep at the wheel of my car. This was a danger to myself and others. It is only by the grace of God I did not hurt myself or someone else. This is what I advise you to do from my experience on preparing for the drive when working on a town. First, eat a good meal and get a good night's sleep before the drive home. Second, carpool with someone else. This way, if you're tired someone else can take over the wheel. Third, if you get tired while driving by yourself pull over at rest stops to do stretches then take a short nap. If you following these tips and advice, you should have no problems when working out of town.

# CHAPTER 13

## Racial Discrimination in the Construction Industry

I would like to start this chapter by making a statement. There is racial discrimination in the construction industry. I am a black man or African American if you prefer. I've been in the construction trade for over 20 years. Many times I had to face and overcome racial prejudice from both white, black and Mexican people to earn my stripes as a carpenter. Racism is, and has always been, a part of this country we call the United States. The best advice I can give is this. As African American men and women it's something we endured since childhood. The good news is you don't have to let this stop you from your dream of becoming a journeyman carpenter or any other thing you want to become. History is full of examples of people who undergo and had to overcome tremendous challenges and became better, stronger people. As African Americans we can consider ourselves privileged.

Young black men hold this country's highest unemployment rate. I need not quote numbers or refer to charts; just tune into the news or google this information if you like. One reason I'm sharing this information with you is that this applies to the construction industry. As black men and women we are often the last hired and the first to be laid off on job-sites. This has been my experience as a working carpenter in the trade. Other races look out for one another. These are the facts. They may respect you and like you as a person but if it comes between them making a decision of keeping you working and putting food on your families table versus them putting food on someone of their own race food table they most likely will let you go first. This is only natural and a basic human response. People who are from the same race watch out for one another.

This used to make me angry and upset. It still bothers me sometimes because it's usually Whites or Mexican foreman and superintendents I must apply for work from. I have built a reputation of being a great carpenter both in the union and outside the union in the San Diego area, but even so I get hired later in the project than my White and Mexican counterparts. At this point you may ask yourself what you can do to combat this. The best thing you can do is to make yourself so valuable as an employee you are impossible or very hard to replace. This is something you can control. Show others you are the best at what you do they will find it hard to just let you go because of your skin color. This has worked for me many times and is what I recommend that you accomplish.

## Overcoming Stereotypes

I don't know when the lie began that black men are lazy and not as skilled as other workers, but *believe me it's not true*. I have had the privileged of working with other colored men in the trades and they are some of the hardest working and highly skilled workers in the construction industry. Black men possess a long history of being skilled workers dating back to before the days of slavery. Many of the Southern Plantations during slavery had black men working as carpenters and iron workers were used to build houses, slave quarters, storehouses for grain, seed and supplies. We were building and repairing fences, wagons and shoeing horses. This is not talked about in school history books or at not least when I went to school. I can even go back further when Egypt had an all-black dynasty of kings responsible for building some of Egypt's first pyramids. One of the oldest lies taught about us is that we were field hands and house servants only.

Never mentioned in the school history books were any of the highly skilled professions that blacks did because this would undermine the lie we were not intelligent and hardworking people. What makes this lie even worse is that other races believe it to be true. Even after over a century removed from slavery people still want to believe the old lie that black people are lazy. When I'm on a job-site I make it my personal mission to prove that this is not the case. I know for a fact that no man can out-work me if I am given a fair opportunity to prove myself. I'm not bragging. This is stating the truth plain and simple. Colored people have always been some of the hardest working people. Slaves cleared the forest for this country's cities and towns. Black workers helped to build this country's infrastructure. Blacks were used to build this nation's first family's house the White House. Former Slaves. We have always been some of this country's hardest workers, it's just that we never were acknowledged or given credit. I think there must be a great awakening, first reminding ourselves that the lie that's been taught about us being lazy was never true. We can change our own and other people's perceptions about ourselves. I myself have been doing this for over the last twenty years. I work so hard that they can't help acknowledging the truth when it is staring them right in the face. I can control my work attitude and my performance as a carpenter. When I continue to outperform other workers they finally are forced to admit that all black people are not lazy and are just as hard working as other when given a fair opportunity.

## Being a Token

Some companies want to look like an equal opportunity employer but are not. They may have one black employee so they can say to themselves or others, "See, we have one minority worker," and then point to the only colored employee they have. I would rather not work for companies like this. Blacks want to be treated right and given the same opportunity as the next man regardless of race or color. I don't want to be the company's token. I'm much better than that, and so are you. If they can't see this, I would much rather work for an employer who does. There are good companies out there who don't care about color or race and evaluate you on performance. Unfortunately, I found out that there are not that many. Some will allow you to stay employed but don't allow you to move up the chain to foreman, superintendent or project manager. My honest opinion is that it's best not to allow yourself to become satisfied in becoming the company's token. If you want more, be more! Having a job is important, but having a dream that is not achieved is a slow painful death.

## Operating Equipment

I heard that equipment operators have one of the highest job satisfaction ratings. It also pays well. They organized their own union and this includes operating a wide range of machinery and equipment both light and heavy. Just like in the other trades, Blacks hold a very low percentage of people represented and employed in the Operators Union. These good paying jobs with high satisfaction ratings are crane operators, earth movers and graders, backhoe, Bobcat and man lift operators. We need more young black men and women applying for and landing these types of good paying positions. We seem to be almost excluded from being able to get these types of jobs. There is one exception. I witnessed a lot of black men hired as cement truck drivers in the San Diego area. Part of the problem that we don't see more blacks working as operators of heavy and light equipment on job-sites is because we don't envision ourselves in these positions, so we don't possess any reference point to start at. Second, there are not enough black mentors coaching these young men and women in what it takes to land these types of jobs.

When I'm walking job-sites I can't help wondering why there are so few Black men and women working in these positions. I know it's not because we would not like to have these good paying jobs. I am only speaking from my experience and what I have witnessed on job-sites during the past twenty years. We seem to be excluded from all the high skilled high-paying opportunities with a few exceptions here and there. This has got to change. If you are a young black man or women, I encourage you to consider joining the operator's union. You must pass the test with a 70% minimum to join the Operators Union. If this is something you would like to do, go for it! Do something today to learn more information or make a contact to make this happen for you. You can start now by looking up the contact information for your local operator's union. When you meet with the union representative ask if they have an open enrollment policy, and also ask what you should do to ready yourself to take the state exam. You can also google the pay and working conditions of equipment operators to get a feel for the job. Talking to people already used in this field is also a great way to gather pay and working condition information of this trade. If this is something you see yourself doing, please do something today to begin this career choice. I would often stay late just to get the opportunity to get on a piece of heavy equipment and learn how to operate the controls. This is how I learned how to operate the bob cat, Gradall, material handler, the back hoe, and the skip loader. I often notice on job-sites one tactic that's used to keep black men from operating even basic equipment is asking, "Have you been certified to use that piece of equipment?" On the surface this sounds like a fair question, until you witness they are not asking other races the same question. These are often the type of politics we must deal with as a race on job-sites.

**Material Mover/Fork Lift/Gradall**

Many white carpenters know how to operate basic equipment. Unfortunately, most blacks are not given the same opportunities to learn and grow in the field. Like Les Brown, one of my favorite motivational speakers would say, "You got to be hungry!" When I was a carpenter apprentice I wanted to learn. Being able to read plans is the key to management positions. When I was in the AGC apprenticeship program one class taught was blueprint reading. What I didn't learn until later out in the field is that being black I would rarely get the opportunity to practice these skills in the field. I soon noticed that whenever I would be on a project my white and Mexican fellow apprentices would be invited in the superintendent or foreman's office to review the job plans, while I would be excluded and told to wait outside for directions from my fellow apprentice. This bothered me a great deal because I had a great thirst for knowledge and was actually eager to learn all I could to advance myself. This went on for the first couple of years until I realized they liked me as a person but had no intentions of teaching me the keys to managing and running work. I would often dig through and retrieve discarded plans from the trash and take them home to study at night. This is how I eventually could read plans. This is what it takes sometimes just to learn something. I must repeat: we are not given or allowed the same opportunities to advance in the construction field as other races.

The playing field has never been level for the black worker. If your experience has been different I'm happy to hear that, but this has been my experience in the trade as a carpenter. Even though you may not always get the same opportunities as your co-workers or shown favor you can still learn to read plans if that is your goal. Asking a question is the key to knowledge. When you see the foreman, superintendent or fellow carpenters reading plans and the opportunity presents itself, ask questions. Most people if approached in the right way will be glad to share their knowledge with you if you show a genuine interest in what they are doing. So ask as many questions as you can if time permits. Listen intently and review and write down what you heard at the end of the day. Then start to practice and apply what you have learned about reading plans as soon as possible. Today at the job-site ask your foreman or superintendent if you can take home a set of plans to study. Share with them what you are trying to accomplish. Tell them you want to become better at your trade and would like the opportunity to get better at reading plans.

This may very well open a new position in the near future for you by showing you would like to become more and are seeking greater responsibility. If you are not able to borrow a set of plans there are always discarded partial plans thrown away for different reasons. These can hold a gold mine of information about the current job including deadline and schedule dates. You can start building your knowledge today. After work each day try to refer to the plan sections and pay close attention to the lay-out dimensions. You will also want to start to memorize symbols. Even though each set of plans have unique symbols many are common and apply to all plans. These things I have suggested you can start doing today to put your career in construction on the fast track to success.

## Lay-Out Work

Construction lay-out is the process of interpreting the information from the plans or Blue Prints such as dimensions, details and elevation views and laying out locations and elevations of foundations, floors, walls and roofs. This knowledge is a key to upward movement in your career as a journeyman carpenter. First you must be competent at reading a set of plans. Remember to study, and practice reading plans daily until you feel confident in your ability to understand and implement this knowledge in the construction field or at your present job-site. Then and only then are you ready to begin building lay-out. Lay-out work is marking the location and elevations of the various components and structures needed to complete the construction of a building. This is a highly skilled position sought out by many carpenters that is always in demand by companies in the construction industry. This is also a position you don't see many black carpenters holding. This knowledge is often protected from older white journeyman carpenters who have been in the trade for years and nurtured in many young white carpenter apprentices.

Very rarely is this skill taught and passed along to black apprentices or journeyman carpenters. As a black carpenter you must be like a sponge, soaking up knowledge in bits and pieces. Often there is less opportunity to practice these skills on job-sites that are run and monopolized by White and Mexican employees in management positions that don't mind giving you a job but might have a problem with you directing crews and running work. Once again you should start today reviewing the job-site plans at any given opportunity and testing your knowledge by pulling out your tape measure to verify locations and dimensions of walls, columns etc. on the job-site compared to the lay-out locations on the plans. You should also become familiar with the operation and set up of the laser level, the builders' level and the laser transit. Mastering these lay-out tools is the key to a management position. See if you can get someone that is knowledgeable in the set up and operation of these lay-out tools to teach you how to set them up and the basics. Then begin to practice this new knowledge and skill when the opportunity presents itself. Often they come with a product manual. You can also take these home to read and study and they will be a great benefit in teaching you the operation and the basics when it comes to these tools. YouTube holds a wealth of information on the use and operation of specialized lay-out processes and tools. Be hungry and willing to learn and the payout will be tremendous.

## Getting Locked in One Position

If you don't plan for advancement in your career in construction you could find your present job position become obsolete, or no longer needed by your employer. Many carpenters end up becoming company foremen or superintendents. If this is one of your long-term goals, you should plan accordingly. How do you accomplish this and keep moving up the career ladder? You must continue to sharpen your skills as a journeyman carpenter starting now. Make the time to take continuing educational trade classes at the BCA, AGC or the Carpenters Union on a regular basis. Call today to see what classes are being offered to you as a member and then schedule the classes. Many classes are canceled if they can't get enough members to enroll and commit to the classes being offered. Make sure your focus and skills are reading plans and building lay-out. These should be at the core of your educational classes and then add other trainings and certificates of completion to complement your plan reading and lay-out classes. If you follow these suggestions, they will give you the greatest opportunity to put you and your career on the fast track to a management position in the construction field.

## Getting Passed Over for Promotions

Let's face it, the world is not fair and neither is the construction industry. Most companies would like to think of themselves as equal opportunity places to work. Very seldom is this the true case. Whites are favored over blacks and men are favored over women. This is a topic most companies or people don't like to address. Let me start with a statement. This book is not about blaming the white man or anyone else for our problems. I am stating the facts as what they are. Being a black person or minority carpenter does not mean you will not be able to get promotions; it means you may have to work twice as hard to get the recognition and promotion that you deserve. True talent and specialized skills are in high demand regardless of race or color. This is a global economy we are living in. If you find that after years of working for your present employer and developing and sharpening your skills, they are unwilling to promote you due to race it may mean it's time to seek out a new employer who is in need of your talent and are willing to let you grow and expand your skills with the company regardless of color or sex.

## Lost Opportunities

Companies that practice discrimination because of race, sex or any other thing on purpose or through their hiring policies are hurting themselves.

In today's global economy and high competition arena specialized skills are in high demand. Employers must seek out and retain talent to stay competitive. Discriminatory practices hurt both the worker and the company. Human potential comes in all races, colors and genders. If you find yourself working for a company that is not promoting you due to your race, first see if you can resolve this issue with the foreman. If he is unreceptive and in your honest opinion is an outright racist, next work your way up the chain of command by discussing this with the superintendent If this is unsuccessful go to the human resources department. Make sure you have plenty of solid evidence before starting this course of action.

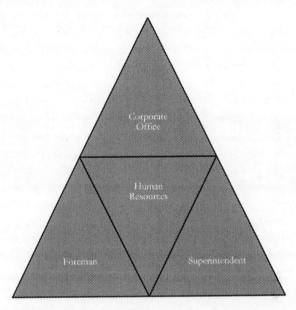

**Chain of Command to File Racial Discrimination Complaint or Grievance.**

If after all your efforts the company as a whole does not wish to promote you because of your race it may be time to move on. I advise to be the bigger person in this situation and don't resort to rage or name calling. This will only serve to help them to justify why they never gave you the opportunity to advance. After some prayer leave the rest in God's hands. When he opens a door no one can close it, and when he closes a door who can open it? Move on and don't look back. God has something better waiting for you.

## Taking on Extra Responsibilities and Leadership

Let me start this paragraph with a statement if you will allow me to. You can't expect to advance in your job or career field if you do only what is expected of you. You must seek out and embrace extra responsibilities and projects if you want the promotions. Most people do only what is expected of them and then have the nerve to complain about why they are not receiving the recognition or promotions they think they deserve. Here is a news flash to people who work like this: promotions go to the workers who arrive early and work late and do much more than is required in their present position. The money you make always follows the value you bring to the organization or company. It's in that order and never the reverse. Money follows value. Repeat this several times until you memorize this and own it. This is a new world and a global economy we live in and this is the secret sauce that will take you where you want to go, not only in your career but in your finances. Start today by asking your employer if you can do more than your present job title requires. Most foreman are not used to this and will gladly give you more projects once the task he assigned you is complete. Be sincere and ask them how you can learn more about the project and contribute more to its completion. Be willing to back this up with hard work and be willing to do whatever it takes to grow into another position of leadership and extra responsibility. Here is another tip: people only see in you what you see in yourself. If you believe with all your heart, mind and soul you are meant to be in a leadership position in your trade, they will see it too. Here is the catch: be willing to take the needed steps and back this up with hard work and unwavering determination, then let no one stop you from fulfilling this purpose.

# CHAPTER 14

## Working Productively

### Working Smart

Carpenters on job-sites are expected to work in a productive manner and this is also something you should continually strive toward. An old saying you will hear often in the trade is "Gett 'er done!" This means completing the task at hand in a fast and efficient manner. So, the question is, "How do I work productively?" When you are given a task to complete, evaluate the total scope of the work, such as where is the closest power source for my tools? What tools am I going to need to complete the job? What materials am I going to need? Where can I find them? How much help is needed to complete the job? How long will this take to complete? What steps do I need to take to insure my safety and that of my co-workers? Do you get the general idea now? Nothing you do can save you more time than good planning. Get in the habit of doing this before each assignment or task and it will pay off tenfold. So let's go over the steps needed to work in a productive professional manner.

### Understanding the Job Task

Step one, make sure you understand the task given to you to complete. Ask plenty of questions for clarification if needed. This will save you the time of having to go back again for more information while working to complete the job. Step two, evaluate and plan the scope of work by finding a power source for operating tools, locating materials, such as 2 x 4 plywood, nails, getting help when needed and planning a safe job. Step three, complete as much lay-out as possible at the same time, such as marking cuts and locations were construction will begin. Step four, gang cut materials when lumber sizes are the same and set up jigs to aid in making your cuts. Gang cutting is the process of stacking material that is the same type or length and flushing the corners before making your cuts. Gang cutting usually refers to cutting more than one piece of lumber at a time. Step five, determine if it make more sense to work from the top down or bottom up. Depending on the job, most of the time it makes more sense to work from the top down, but in some circumstances working from the bottom up may make more sense. After experience in the trade you will have to make this decision to see what method is more effective and works out the best. Monitor progress and re-evaluate when necessary to meet deadlines. Get in the habit of always re-evaluating your work and processes. Just like professional teams and athletes keep reviewing the instant replay over and over to look for mistakes and decide where improvements can be made, you as a professional carpenter should be doing the same thing on a weekly basis to stay at the top of your game.

## Lay-Out Work

One of the tricks of the trade that was taught to me was when cutting materials is to complete all you lay-out at once if possible. What does that mean? For an example, let's say you and another carpenter are working together building something out of wood. He asks you to cut several rips of plywood and gives you the numbers. The first thing I do is repeat the numbers or dimensions back to him to make sure there are no misunderstandings about what numbers he has giving me. Afterwards, I write them down on a piece of paper or a scrap piece of wood if there is no paper handy. Then if the numbers are the same and he may need many pieces you can use the production cutting method. You stack several pieces of lumber on top of each other, making sure the corners are flush. Mark your lay-out for the cuts on the top sheet. Cut only as much material as the thickness of the blade. Most standard skill saws have a 7½ in. blade and can't cut any deeper than 3½ inches at one time. This means it's best not to attempt to cut more than two 4 x 8 sheets of plywood stacked on top of each other at a time if the thickness dimension is ¾ inch ply. Overloading the motor of an electric rip saw can burn out the motor. Even though it might be possible to try and rip three sheets of ¾ inch plywood at one time, I don't recommend this for the reasons I just stated. Besides, your rips will be cleaner and the saw works much better if the blade is not fully buried in the material while cutting.

When stacking plywood for the production cutting method, make sure that you nail opposite corners first to keep the ends flush and keep the material from shifting while cutting. When production cutting 2 x 4, stepping on the material firmly is often enough to keep the ends flush and the lumber from shifting. Just use common sense with this method; if the material is moving or if the corners are not flush, act accordingly. When cutting 4 x 4 post material gently roll the lumber while cutting, making sure you maintain a firm grip during this process. Also make sure that the cut extends beyond the cutting table or surface, allowing the lumber to drop freely after making your cuts. When cutting wood 4 x 4 post begin first by marking a square line around your material. Always try to cut all of your material for a project at once if possible. This will cut down on running back and forth to the saw and save you time. Remember the golden rule for carpenters: measure twice and cut once. This is extremely important and will save money due to making a bad cut and having to re-purchase or search for additional lumber after making a bad cut. Another timesaving method is memorizing where your tools are in your carpenter bags. You should be able to reach for and find any tool without much thought. You can achieve this by returning tools after use to the same location. I often experiment with what is the best location for my hand tools, especially when purchasing a different set of bags.

**Carpenter Working with a Full Set of Carpenter Bags.**

There is a tremendous selection of manufacturers that make carpenter bags. They also come in a wide variety of shapes, sizes and materials. Make certain the bags you purchase will be tailored to the specific needs of the job. Each specialty of carpentry requires a different set of tools for the construction task to be performed. Make sure the bags you purchase have enough pockets and holders to carry the tools you are going to carry is the general rule that I follow. Keep your work area clean and organized. This is something often overlooked by carpenters. A clean work environment is pleasant to work at and is much safer for you and your co-workers. When tools are well organized they are easy to locate and tend to be better cared for. Organized materials can be inventoried and easily found when needed, saving both time and money. Now that you have all the necessary information go out there, be a professional and have a productive working career.

# CHAPTER 15

# Construction Technology for the New Millennium

Let's start this chapter with a short history lesson on how black men and women have contributed to some of the world's greatest buildings and structures. Construction technology is always changing and advancing. Since the beginning of time men have gotten together to build things, from Noah's Ark in the Bible to the Black Pharaohs of AFRICA and EGYPT. For 75 years Nubian Kings ruled over ancient Egypt, reunifying the country and building one of the greatest empires the world had ever seen at that time. In the 25th Dynasty of Egypt our black ancestors were no strangers to the most advanced building practices and techniques. It was during the 25th Dynasty that the Nile Valley saw the first widespread construction of the pyramids. Moving forward to America in 1792, slave labor helped cut the rough stone that was later dressed for the walls of the White House. Slave carpenters Ben, Daniel, and Peter were also employed by their owners. Slaves were likely involved in all aspects of construction, including masonry, rafting, glazing, and painting. And slaves most likely had to shoulder alone the grueling work of sawing logs and stones.

Slave crews also toiled at the marble and sandstone quarries that provided the stone to face the structure, lonely, grueling work with bleak living conditions in rural Virginia and elsewhere. "Keep the yearly hirelings at work from sunrise to sunset, particularly the Negros," the commissioners wrote to quarry operator Williams O' Neal in 1794. Most of the slaves who worked on the Capitol are known by first name at best, but one particular slave Philip Reid achieved some renown as an individual. He was a slave laborer for Clark Mills, who was hired to cast the statue of freedom, the Capitol's crowning feature. The government paid Reid $ 1.25 a day for his work.

The statue, a draped female figure holding a sheathed sword in one hand and a laurel wreath in the other, stands atop the Capitol dome 288 feet above the site of President Obama's swearing in.

## Green Building

When did designers first become interested in building green homes? Today, we are still at the beginning of the construction movement, as solar panels, renewable materials, and efficient design are still being introduced into the mainstream. Tomorrow, green building could be the norm.

## When Did Green Building Begin?

Individuals and companies have only been building green homes for the past 30-plus years; still, within that time, the green movement has been constantly growing. The history of green building dates back much further than the 1970s, it was in the early part of the industrial revolution the transformation of solar energy into electrical energy. Around this time, and in the late 1800s to the early 1900s a number of solar power plants were built to utilize the sun's energy for steam power. Then, in the 1950s solar energy was used on an extremely small-scale, making way for the solar panel solution 20 years later. During the energy crisis of the 1970s, green building moved from research and development to reality. Builders and designers were looking for ways to reduce the reliance of buildings and homes on fossil fuels. Solar panels were used to make more environmentally friendly homes although only in very small numbers due to high initial costs. Since then, developers have been able to construct more efficient and less expensive solar panels, making solar energy more of a reality. Also, during this transition period, designers and consumers started wondering if solar panels can make buildings more efficient, lower energy bills, and reduce the negative impact on the environment. What other steps can be taken to build even greener homes? Now, ECO construction involves so much more than simply using solar panels.

## Considerations

Aside from harnessing the earth's richest energy source, sunlight is known as and designers examine a number of issues to make a building Eco-friendly. Building materials are a huge concern. Even today, the building industry of the United States uses up to 40% of all raw materials. Any reduction through the use of sustainable, recycled materials will have a huge impact on resource preservation. Durability is another issue; if environmentally framing materials need to be replaced frequently then they become less and less efficient.

Good location is a central component for eco construction. Homes should be close to the community or public transportation to reduce the need for driving in the neighborhood space that will not harm the surrounding environment. Green homes should also be designed to encourage recycling, manage water use, and minimize energy use.

## What Does the Future Hold for Building Green?

Today, green design is still a relatively new concept and the history of green building only goes back a few decades. This however is changing; the movement will inevitably grow, not just because consumers want to own more environmentally, friendly, safer and cleaner homes for their families, but because society will be dependent on the efficiency and long-term expense reduction of building green homes. Those who have experience with green building and design, either through their own home or business or through working in the industry, have set an example of benefits of the full transformation, saving money, energy and reducing waste.

## The Solar Industry

Solar power, for all its promises and contention, still remains very expensive and dollar for dollar is more expensive than fossil fuels. Housing installing solar panels and the industry as a whole continues to expand, but the manufacturing side remains in the dumps because supply far exceeds demand. Their weak demand may be slowing innovation, but improvements continue. Recently solar panels energy cost something like 50¢ per watt and there's talk of hitting 30¢ per watt. The US Dept. of Energy has set a goal of reaching less than a dollar a watt not just for solar panels, but for complete insulation systems by 2020. The Green's lab built a solar cell in the 1990s that set a record efficiency for the silicon solar cells, a record that stands to this day.

Meanwhile, researchers at the national renewable energy laboratory have made flexible solar cells on a new type of glass from Corning called windows glass, which is thin and can be rolled up. This type of solar cell is the only current challenger to silicon in terms of large-scale production. These new construction technologies can be game changers for most carpenters. You should learn as much as you can and stay on top of these new technologies to compete for the job-sites that will be created in the next millennia.

# CHAPTER 16

## Certifications and Certificates

Certifications and continuing training are available to all carpenter apprentices and journeyman carpenters who need certifications to operate special equipment, need further trainings to recognize certain hazards, and special skills to perform tasks and assignments. Certificates are awarded after completing a curriculum of study or program that is approved by a governing body that set certain standards of achievement for completing a course of study. The major difference between the two are that certifications are for a certain period. Then after that time period they must be up-dated or the training taken again to keep current with all the new developments and training in the construction industry. To sum it up, they have a shelf life that ends after a certain period. Certificates have no shelf life. They are awarded for completing an area of study or training and are awarded at a completion ceremony recognizing the accomplishment. As a professional tradesman you should seek to gain as many relevant trainings and certifications as needed to perform you job in a professional and safe manner.

Certifications and certificates of completion will also help open doors that might not be available for you if had not completed the trainings. Every carpenter especially *blacks and minority workers* need every possible advantage to remain competitive in today's job market. There are trainings, certifications, and certificates offered in almost every area of construction— areas like equipment operation, safety, welding, rigging, storm water protection, and so on. Usually the Black Contractors Association, the Carpenters Union, and the Associated General Contractors of America offer classes some free others for a fee to gain and receive certifications and certificates of completion. Many colleges and adult continuing education programs also offer trainings where you can receive educational credits for completing certification and certificate trainings. Carlton Sheets a real estate guru made an interesting statement that I will never forget. He said you should set aside money on a regular basis to be able to afford trainings as they may become available. He also stated that this is like making an investment in yourself and your future. I recommend that you follow his advice in this area. The AGC offers trainings in storm water prevention, fork lift certification, rigger and signal person, confined spaces and many more classes and trainings. Contact your local AGC charter for starting dates, fees and enrollment.

# CHAPTER 17

---

# Preparing for the Contractor's Exam

Let me start by saying that becoming a contractor is the next logical step if you choose to open your own business in construction. As a black man I would love to see many more of our race not only getting their contractor's license but also hiring black youth and passing on construction building skills to the next generation. Let's not sugarcoat this: major black contracting companies are in short supply in America. We need more black men and women thinking about and getting their contract license. Just who can become a licensed contractor? For starters you must be at least 18 years old and must possess the experience and skills to manage and supervise in the daily activities of construction.

## General Requirements

Why must you be licensed as a contractor? If you plan to construct or alter a building, road or other structure in California with a total cost of labor and materials on one, or more than one project that is $500 dollars or more, you must have a contractor's license. It's that simple. Passing the contractors' exam is not hard. It basically comes down to making a personal commitment to yourself. You must start by asking yourself these questions. How much do I want to be a contractor? What is the payoff in personal satisfaction, recognition, and financial gain? What am I willing to sacrifice to achieve this goal? How much am I willing to study? Questions like these will shed light on your personal desire and motivation before wasted time and effort are made.

## Experience Requirements

You are required to take a trade and/or law examination for licensure. What type of experience is required to receive your license? You must have at least four years of experience to qualify to take the California State Exam. Credit for experience is given only for experience at the journeyman level or as a foreman. What is journeyed-level experience? Journeyman carpenter experience applies to a person who has completed an apprenticeship program or is an experienced worker, not a trainee, and is fully qualified and able to perform a specific trade without supervision by a supervising employee, contractor, or as an owner builder. All experience claims must be verified by a qualified and responsible person such as a homeowner, an employer, fellow employee, contractor, union representative, building inspector, architect, or engineer. Anyone verifying your experience must have firsthand knowledge of your claim.

## CSLB Licensing Classifications

For the purpose of classification, the contract in business includes any or all of the following branches;

(A) General Engineering Contractor
(B) General Building Contractor
(C) Specialty Contractor

## Content of the Examination

The General Building (B) Examination is divided into five major sections.

1. **Planning and Estimating (24%)**

   - Scope of work and code compliance
   - Design and construction error identification
   - Shop drawings, plans, and specifications
   - Field inspections performance
   - Coordination of project
   - Cost estimation for materials, equipment, and labor

2. **Framing and Structural Components (23%)**

- Subfloor and wall framing
- Roof framing
- Seismic load requirements
- Decks
- Siding and stucco

3. **Core Trades (26%)**

- Plumbing
- Electrical
- HVAC
- Concrete
- Earthwork and surveying
- Insulation, acoustical, and weather proofing
- Roofing

4. **Finish Trades (19%)**

- Painting, staining, coating, and interior wall covering
- Tile and stone
- Floor covering
- Cabinetry and millwork
- Plaster, drywall, and ceilings, windows, skylights, and doors
- Landscaping

5. **Safety (8%)**

- Personnel safety
- Transportation and traffic control
- Environmental safety

## Test Site Policy

When you go to take the contractor's exam it will be a closed book examination. No reference materials may be used during the examination.

The contractor's exam is a multiple-choice test. Some questions require mathematical computations. Plenty of time is provided to answer all examination questions, so be sure to read each question completely and carefully before selecting the best possible answer to each question.

There are many schools that will help get you ready to take and pass the state contractors' exam. If this is your choice take the time to do the research and make sure they are a reputable school that delivers on their promises. There are also many books you can purchase online or at book stores that will help get you ready to pass the state contractors' exam. No matter which route you take the personal commitment to receive your license must come from you.

# CHAPTER 18

## Continue Learning

### Asking Questions

First let me state that there is no such thing as a stupid question. No one is born with knowledge in their current occupation. All learning starts with questions like why, what, and how. When I was a carpenter apprentice, I would question everything I came across such as why do we do it this way? How is the best way to start? What is that you are working on? By asking questions like this I was able to understand the processes involved in completing a task or project. If I had never begun with asking a question, I would not have understood why things were done a certain way and probably would have underestimated its importance or even worst lost interest and maybe given up. Questions free the mind and spark interest. That is why children at a very young age are always asking why. Unfortunately, as we grow older we begin to ask fewer questions from the fear of looking stupid in front of our peers. Raising questions also can help you see the big picture. In construction it is easy to get side tracked in a project and lose track of the big picture. What I mean by the big picture is the ultimate result or goal you are trying to accomplish. You must ask questions to find out and understand what this is. The more questions you ask about a project the greater your understanding becomes. Engineers often take this approach by asking all the tough questions before coming up with a design or prototype for a new product. Don't be afraid to say, "Can you please repeat that?" or "I did not get that last point." If you start doing this today, you will be ahead of your competition. Posing the right questions will help you discover solutions. NASA engineers do it and so should you. Get in the practice of writing down well thought out questions and seek people out who can answer these, or at least point you in the right direction. By developing this habit today, you will increase your knowledge in a subject by leaps and bounds. The solutions often lie in asking and working out the answers to the right questions. This is one of the secrets to Forward thinking and leadership. Plus, this is something you can start to practice now.

## Learning from Journeyman Carpenters

Journeyman carpenters can teach you a lot about construction and cut your learning curve about something in half. For starters they have years of experience under their belts out in the field of hands-on experience that cannot be easily replaced. For someone new to the construction trade one of the greatest gifts and learning opportunities will come to you if you get the chance to pair up with an older carpenter. Learning the tricks of the trade takes years of experience to gain and master. This is something that an experienced carpenter can help you with. Most are well rounded in the construction trade as a whole. Carpenters of an earlier time period had less specialization and usually knew how to build a structure from the ground up to the finishes. Today specialized tradesmen only master one aspect of the building. You should think of yourself like a sponge when giving the opportunity to work with an older tradesman, soaking up as much information and knowledge as possible. Journeyman carpenters also tend to be problem solvers. They have been in the field for a long period of time and have probably been confronted and challenged with many difficult building situations and challenges. They most likely have developed a logical process of identifying and solving problems. This is a skill that will always be in high demand. Getting into this field you should learn from them and develop your own unique style of approaching and solving construction related problems. This is something you could easily start on today. Identify the problem and then have a brainstorm session to come up with solutions.

## Learning from Laborers

Laborers can often be a valuable source of learning when it comes to construction. They have many important jobs in the completion of a building and construction project. Their main responsibilities when it comes to commercial construction is stripping and organizing materials, getting the materials to carpenters and banded for transport, back to rental companies, pouring and finishing concrete and keeping the construction site clean and orderly. Journeyman laborers are also responsible for pouring concrete. Many can finish concrete as well. If you want to learn about what it takes to get ready for a major concrete pour you would do well to get advice on the ins and outs from a journeyman labor. Many of them have been in the trade for years and have been involved in many concrete pours. They are responsible for making sure the concrete is poured to the proper height set by pouring strips that carpenters install. They often set up the lighting and operate vibrators that help the mixed concrete settle in the forms and prevent rock pockets.

**Laborer Apprentice Directing Traffic**

Laborers also are responsible for stripping concrete forms in a safe manner. This can take years to master. Many laborers are better than carpenters when it comes to stripping forms due to more time spent in this area and experience. Some forms can be very high and dangerous to strip. Many times only very experienced laborers can ensure that this operation goes safely and efficiently. Some forms can be as high as 50 feet from the ground, making the stripping of these forms extremely challenging, that's why many are extremely self-confident in their abilities and skills. Many carpenters start as laborers. This is a good way of learning the trade from the ground up, then as your skills and confidence increase you can branch out into other positions or trades. Many laborers can operate specialized equipment to help them in their task such as scissor lifts or man lifts. These often aid them when stripping high forms.

**Labor Removing Re-Shores During Stripping Operation**

If this is an occupation that interests you, you can start today by looking up on the internet where the nearest Laborers Union hall is, or better yet talk to a laborer on a job-site to get more detailed information about this career path.

## How Can Mistake Be the Greatest Teachers?

First let me start by saying everyone makes mistakes. It's part of being human. No one is perfect. One of the greatest lessons you can learn when making a mistake is what not to do. There is a saying that is often used in 12-step programs: "Insanity is doing the same thing over and over again and expecting different results." When you make a mistake you have just learned that the approach you are using is not working. This can save time and money if this lesson is learned quickly. Many people go on making that same mistake over and over again. You should change your approach if something you are trying to accomplish is not working. Changing something is the key to discovering if something is going to work or not. A new approach can mean just shaking things up. Produce a brainstorming session to come up with multiple solutions to the problem. Then you can eliminate the ridiculous and far-fetched solutions and focus on the ones that make the most sense. Try this today if you have a problem in your work or personal life. This is a great way of putting this new problem-solving skill into practice. Sometimes just getting away from a problem or taking a break will bring new insight and a fresh perspective. Often when returning to the problem the answer will come to you.

What is the best way to memorize new trade processes and secrets? Memorizing new knowledge and construction techniques can be quite challenging. Fortunately, there are many tools to aid you in accomplishing this task. One of my favorite tools I have used to aid me in memorizing something new has been the use of *flash cards*. Their low cost and small size makes them ideal for on-the-spot review and memorizing of new subjects, words and techniques. You can purchase a set of 25-100 at almost any office supply store. You write the subject matter on one side and the details, definitions or the process on the opposite side, then whenever you have some free time you bring them out for a quick review session. The more you review the better the memory you will have. After a few weeks you won't need them for the new subject matter at all if you review often during each day.

I advise that you stop by an office supply store and purchase some today and start writing down what you are trying to learn. You will be amazed how much information you can recall if you start exercising your memory and use this tool on a daily basis. The second tool I would like to share with you is to get into the habit of carrying a pocket sized note pad with you to write down new information you would like to retain and review at a later date. I have about ten legal sized note pads on many subjects of interest that I can review if needed. This has been of great benefit to me over the years and continues to help me when I would like to review or retain information. This is something you can also start to do to retain your knowledge on a given subject. Even the writing process itself helps us to memorize and retain new information. The last thing I would like to touch on in the area of memorizing construction trade secrets and techniques is that you have to practice and put new skills into use out in the field to own it and really retain this new information. We learn best by taking notes then seeing and doing. This is a three-dimensional process to really learning something new. Let's review the learning process. First see something done, then take plenty of good notes for later review and study, then practice this new information in the field. Only after this process do you truly own this new skill or information.

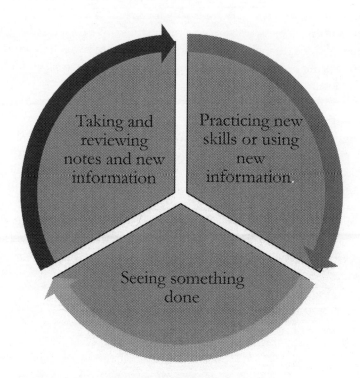

**The Learning Process**

**YouTube videos** are one of the greatest free teaching tools available today. You can literally watch and learn from any subject for free on YouTube. That is amazing when you think about it. People during history and even still today pay thousands of dollars for this learning privilege. Today you can arrange an instructor in front of you in seconds to help teach you and understand any subject ever studied or written about. Whenever I bid on construction jobs I will often review these YouTube videos to review or learn about something I have never done before. Once you learn the safe operation of tools and gain the basic principle and methods of construction, all you need is to see something constructed and you will be able to follow the instructions and build the same thing as a journeyman carpenter or contractor. Referring back to the pie chart above, seeing is the foundation of learning. Unlike language, where words are used to transfer information and ideas, you can learn how to do something from anyone even if they speak a different language from you. YouTube is an amazing free learning tool that you should take full advantage of. Unlike traditional education classrooms you can watch a YouTube video at any time of the night or day in your pajamas. What other place can you accomplish all this for free? YouTube is always free, perfect for people that are cash strapped or on a low income. For blacks and minorities, we are often not able to participate in educational programs due to finance or low income. This is your opportunity to learn regardless of cost. The more you know the more value you can contribute and the greater the income you will receive. The right education is still the key but unlike in the past there are no financial barriers to keep you from participating.

**ROP** is also a great place to get free or low-cost occupational training to further your career. They are officially referred to as the Regional Occupational Program. San Diego, the city where I am from, has the largest in the state. They have been offering low-cost training programs since 1969. The program is accredited by the Western Association of Schools and Colleges. ROP courses are available to anyone aged 16 and up and they offer over 265 tuition-free courses every year. They even offer college credit classes but they may require a payment or a tuition fee. The good news is that all ROP courses are available as a tuition-free class. This is another learning opportunity that blacks or minorities should be taking full advantage of. Today there is simply no excuse that you can give as to why you can't afford to further your occupational education to learn more about their mission and the classes they offer. Please visit their website at San Diego County ROP Website: http://www.sdcoe.net/rop/

The continuing Adult Education Centers sponsored by the college educational system also like ROP offer hundreds of tuition-free occupational and general education classes. Many of these are in the building trades and could be of great benefit in helping you advance and further your education. I never recommend anything that I have myself not used. I have personally taken many of these free courses for everything from accounting and bookkeeping to computer programs and typing classes. I have always known that free education is something I could not afford to pass on, as a result I received the opportunity to work in several fields from construction, landscaping, real estate and now book author, all because I was always ready and willing to take advantage of free education classes and programs. There are so many resources and free programs available nowadays that lack of funds is no longer an excuse.

San Diego County ROP Website: http://www.sdcoe.net/rop/

## Low-cost Books

I started when I was a carpenter apprentice to build a library of low-cost books on carpentry and the different trades in construction. This is one of the best decisions I believe I have ever made to further my understanding and knowledge of construction. I will always believe that knowledge is power. Today the price of printed books continues to fall due to more people reading and accessing e-books and information on the internet. I think this is a tremendous opportunity to build a book library on a low budget. I don't ever remember spending more than 40 bucks on any book and most of my books cost just a few dollars. For the cost of a fast food meal I can purchase three or four books that can help me bid my next job that may bring in hundreds of dollars in return for my small investment. That is leveraging your money for the future. If you just spent 10-20 dollars a month purchasing books from thrift store or swap meets about carpentry or the construction trade, you would own a full library of knowledge you could refer to that will help you land jobs. Sometimes I just enjoy learning about something I have never done or had the chance to do before. I have a library to refer to whenever I feel the need to learn something new about a construction project. If you are on a low budget this is a great way of investing in your education and future. What we need as black people is a new attitude about what is valuable and what deserves our attention and dollars. If we don't want to be forever trying to play catch up with other races this is a basic concept we must understand. What better way to leverage today's dollars for the benefit of your education and future than building a library of low-cost books?

**The internet** is also another learning resource. There are so many opportunities to connect with others in the trades with similar interest like your own, like the National Black Contractors Association and the Black Carpenters Association. There are countless opportunities to find employment and sell your services, like Craigslist, where I was able to advertise my services as a carpenter and generate enough work to take care of me and my family when the work in the Carpenters Union slowed down. I could write a whole book on just the opportunities created by the internet. The focus of this book is just to remind you of its potential to literally change your life with learning opportunities, the many ways to make meaningful and lasting connections on Facebook, LinkedIn and twitter plus countless others social media web sites, as well as the countless opportunities to create business and advertise your services. Take the time to explore these possibilities.

Were you aware that the Home Depot offers free classes for do it yourselfers on everything from tiling to landscaping? Check out their website for locations and classes offered in your local area.

## Google Books

Google Books is also an amazing resource when it comes to learning about any subject. This past year I read "The Negro in Business" written by Booker T. Washington. I was stunned at all the progress black people had made in business after the Civil War and how we suffer from a tremendous loss of the black businesses like banks and grocery stores we once owned due to the 1921 Oklahoma Riots in Tulsa. The point is I never would have learned this information had it not been for Google Books. They possess hundreds of books on construction, black business ownership and any other subject that may interest you. I don't own a huge bank account so most of my books I read on Google Books are completely free like the one I just shared with you. We are very fortunate to be living in these times where you can get free unbiased access to information. It was a very different story in my parents' generation when information was restricted and whitewashed. I'm not going to sugar coat this. What I mean by that last comment is they were not told the whole story, or were outright lied to about many subjects especially history and the contributions the black race has made as a whole to the advancement of civilization. Today no one has complete control of all the information thanks to the internet. The sad part is now that all this information is available, few people are taking full advantage of this recent development. Getting back to the current topic, I have built a library of about one hundred books in my Google Books Account on the construction field, real estate, self-development and black history.

## Learning to Use a Construction Calculator

Every journeyman carpenter should own and know how to use a construction calculator. This tool can save you both money and time because of the benefits. This is something that you should strive to master. Construction calculators help you calculate materials, do math formulas, figure out radius for circles, determine rafter lengths and provide countless other time saving functions. Construction is an industry where time is money. Today's construction professional can't compete without the use of this handy pocket tool. They usually come with a small operators manual and guide to its operation. Study this and practice the calculations in the field often to master its operation. Today's black carpenter needs every advantage at his or her disposal to help level the playing field. By becoming familiar with the use and operation of the construction calculator you will be able to gain the upper hand by having estimates that are accurate and fast, which often makes the difference between making money or losing money for a carpenter bidding work or a general contractor doing material take-offs.

## Glossary of construction terms

The glossary contains many of the more general building terms.

Airway. A space between the roof insulation and the roof awards, for movement of air.

Anchor bolts. Bolts use to secure a wood sill or plate to concrete or to masonry flooring on walls.

Apron. The visible trim of window, placed against the wall that immediately beneath the stool.

Attic ventilators. Screen openings provided to ventilate attic spaces. They're located in the soffit area as inlet ventilators and in the gable end or along the ridge as longer range of outlet ventilators. Attic ventilators can also be powered using fans as an exhaust system.

Astragal. Trim (often shaped) that covers the common joint of contiguous windows.

Backband. A simple molding sometimes used as a decorative feature around the outer edge of a plane rectangular casting.

Back fill. The replacement of excavated earth in a trench around and against a basement foundation.

Balusters. Usually, small vertical members in a railing used between a top rail and stair treads or a bottom rail.

Balustrade. In assembly of balusters, top rail, and sometimes bottom rail; used on the edge of stairs, balconies, and porches.

Barge boards. A decorative board covering for a projecting rafter (fly rafter) of the gable end. At the cornice, this number is called fascia board.

Base board. A board place at the base of a wall, next to the floor, to properly finish the joint between the floor and wall surface.

Base molding. Molding used to trim the upper edge of a baseboard.

Batten. A narrow strip of wood used a cover a joint or a decorative vertical member over plywood or a wide board.

Batter board. One of a pair of horizontal boards nailed to posts set at the corners of an excavation, used to indicate a desired level; a fastening for stretched strings to indicate outlines of foundation walls.

Bay. The space between any pair of rafters, studs, or joists.

Bay window. Any window space projecting outward from the walls of a building, either rectangular or polygonal in plan.

Beam. A structural member, usually horizontal, that supports a load.

Bearing partition. A partition the supports a vertical load in addition to its own weight.

Bearing wall. A wall that supports vertical load in addition to its own weight.

Blind-nailing. Nailing in such a way that that nail-heads are not visible on the face of the work, usually through the tongue of match boards.

Blind stop. A rectangular molding, usually ¾ in. x 11/8 in. or more in width, used in assembling a window frame. Serves as a stop for storm and screen or combination windows in two resists air infiltration.

Blocking. Dimension lumber added to bolster a nailing point.

Board lumber. Yard lumber, usually 1-inch-thick is always less than 2 inches thick, or wider.

Boiled linseed oil. Linseed oil in which enough lead, manganese or cobalt salts have been incorporated to make the oil harden more rapidly than spreading thin coats.

Bolster. A short horizontal timber or steel beam on top of the column that spreads the load of beams or girders.

Boston ridge. Asphalt or wood shingles applied at the ridge or the hips of a roof as a finish.

Brace. An inclined piece of framing lumber applied to walls or floors to stiffen the structure. Often used on walls as a temporary bracing until framing and sheathing is complete.

Brick veneer. A facing of brick laid against and fastened to sheathing of frame wall or tile wall construction.

Bridging, cross-bridging. A small wood and metal member inserted in the diagonal position between the floor joists at mid-span to act both as tension and as compression members for the purpose of bracing the joist is spreading the action of loads. Solid bridging or blocking uses lengths of dimensional lumber for similar effects.

Built-up roof. A roofing composed of 3 to 5 layers of asphalt felt laminated with coal tar, pitch, or asphalt. The top is finished with crushed slag or gravel. Generally used on flat or low-pitched roofs.

Butt joints. The junction where the ends of two timbers or other members meet in a square-cut joint.

Cant strip. A triangular piece of lumber used at the junction of a flat deck and the wall to prevent cracking of the roofing applied over it and to aid water runoff.

Cap. The upper member of the column, pilaster, door cornice, molding, and so on.

Casement frames and sash. Frames of wood or metal enclosing part or all of the sash, which can be opened by means of hinges affixed to two of the vertical edges.

Casing. Molding of various widths and thickness, used to trim door and window openings.

Checking. Fissures that appear with age and many exterior materials and pain coatings.

Collar beam. Members connecting opposite roof rafters that stiffen the roof structure, also called collar ties.

Column. In architecture, a perpendicular supporting member, circular or rectangular in section, usually consisting of a base, shaft and capital. In engineering, a vertical structure compression member would support loads acting in the direction of its longitude axis.

Combination doors, windows. Combination doors and windows that provide winter insulation and summer protection and often have self-storing are removable glass and screen inserts.

Condensation. In a building, beads, drops of water, or frost that can accumulate on the inside of the exterior covering of a building when warm, moisture-laden air from the interior reaches a point where it can no longer hold moisture.

Construction, frame. A type of construction in which the structural parts are woods or a material that is supported by wood frame.

Corbel out. To build out one or more courses of brick or stone from the face of a wall to support overhead of some of the elements above.

Corner bead. A strip of one sheet metal placed on drywall or plaster corners as the reinforcement. Also, a strip of wood finish, ¾ round of angular, placed over plaster corner for protection.

Corner boards. Trim on the exterior corners of a house; the ends of the siding often abut the corner boards.

Corner braces. Diagonal braces at the corner of the frame structure, used to stiffen and straighten a wall.

Cornerite. Metal-mesh lath cut in strips and bent at a right angle. Used in the interior corners of a wall and ceilings on lath to prevent cracking of plaster.

Cornice. Overhanging of a pitched at the eve line, usually consisting of fascia board, a soffit (for a closed cornice) and appropriate molding. On a flat roofed structure, the cornice is often the uppermost part of the roof where it overhangs the front of the house.

Counterflashing. Two pieces of flashing commonly used on chimneys at the roofline to cover single flashing and to prevent moisture from entering.

Cove molding. A molding with a concave face, use as trim to finish interior corners.

Crawl space. A shallow space between the living quarters of a basement house, normally enclosed by foundation walls.

Cricket. A small drainage-diverting roof structure of single or double slope, placed at the junction or large surface that meets an angle, such as a book a chimney. Sometimes called a "saddle."

Crown molding. A molding used at a cornice or wherever an interior angle is to the cover; also a complex molding at the top of an interior wall.

Curtain wall. A non-bearing wall.

Dado. A rectangular groove, usually across the width of a board or plank.

Deck paint. An enamel with a high degree of resistance to wear, designed for use on such services as porch floors.

Dew point. The temperature at which a vapor begins to condense as a liquid.

Dimensional lumber. Usually lumber 2 inches thick but not thicker than 5 inches, and 2 inches or wider. The term covers joists, rafters, studs, planks, and small timbers.

Doorjamb, interior. The surrounding frame of a door; consist of two upright pieces, called "side jambs," and a horizontal head, or the head jamb.

Dormer. The opening in a sloping roof, the framing of which protrudes, forming vertical walls suitable for windows and other openings.

Downspout. A pipe, usually of metal, for carrying rainwater from roof gutters.

Drip cap. A molding placed on the exterior top side of a door or window frame, causing water to drip beyond the frame.

Drip edge. A metal edge projecting over other parts, especially along the edges of the roofs for throwing off water.

Drip kerfs. A groove under a sill that allows water to drip free from the surface rather than clinging and running down the face of the house.

Drywall. Interior covering material, usually gypsum board, applied in large sheets or panels. Commonly called "Sheetrock," a major brand.

Ducts. Round or rectangular metal pipes for distributing warm air from a heating plant to rooms, or the air from an air conditioning device.

Eave. The margin, or lower part of a roof, which projects over a wall.

Face-nailing. Nailing perpendicular to the surface or the junction of two pieces that are joined. Also called direct nailing.

Fascia. A flat board, band, or face sometimes used alone, though usually in combination with moldings; most often located out the outer face of the cornice.

Field. Any relative flat, unobstructed expanse of building material.

Finish, natural. A transparent finish that largely maintains an original color or grain of wood. Natural finishes are usually provided by sealers, oils, varnishes, water repellent preservatives and similar materials.

Fire stop. Located in the frame wall, usually consisting of 2 x 4, cross blocking between studs; impedes spread of fire and smoke.

Flashing. Sheet metal or other material used in roof and wall construction to protect the building from water seepage.

Flat paint. An interior paint that contains a high proportion of pigment; dries to a flat lusterless finish.

Flue. Fire clay or terra-cotta lines in the chimney though which smoke, gases and fumes ascend. Each passage is called the "flue." The flues, together with other parts and the surrounding masonry, constitute a chimney.

Fly rafters. End rafters of a gable overhanging supported by roof sheeting and lookouts.

Footing. A masonry section, usually concrete, in a rectangular form wider than the bottom of the foundation wall or pier it supports.

Foundation. The supporting portion of a structure below the first floor of construction, or below grade (ground level) including footings.

Frieze. In house construction, a horizontal member connecting the top of the siding with the soffit of the cornice.

Frost line. The depth of frost penetration in the soil.

Furring. Strips of wood or metal applied to a wall or another surface to even it and, normally, to serve as a fastening base for finish material.

Gable. In house construction, the portion of the roof above the eave line or a double sloped roof.

Gable end. An end wall that has a gable.

Girder. A large, or the principle, beam of wood or steel used to support concentrated loads, such as joist ends, along its length.

Gloss. Paint or enamel that contains a relatively low portion of pigment and dries to a sheen or luster.

Grain. The direction, size, arrangement, appearance, and quality of the fibers of a piece of wood.

Grout. Mortar made of such a consistency by adding water that it will flow into the joints and cavities of masonry work, filling them. In tiling, a specialized mortar that seals off joints between tiles.

Gusset. A flat board, plywood, or similar member used to provide a connection at the intersection of wood members, commonly used as wood-truss joints.

Gutter. A shallow channel of metal or wood sent below and along the eaves of a house to catch and carry rainwater away from the roof.

Header. (1) A beam placed perpendicular to joists, to which joists are nailed in framing for chimney, stairway, or some other opening. (2) A beam above a door or window opening. (3) In floor framing, the outermost joist running perpendicular to the others in the grid.

Hip. The external angle formed by the meeting of two sloping sides of a roof.

I beam. A steel beam with a cross section resembling the letter "I."

Insulation, thermal. Any material high in resistance to heat transmission that, when placed in walls, ceiling, or floors of the structure, reduces the rate of heat flow.

Interior finish. Materials used to cover interior framed areas, or materials of walls and ceilings.

Jack rafter. A rafter that spans the distance from the wall plate to the hip, measured from the valley to the ridge.

Jamb. The side elements of a door of a window frame.

Joint. The space between adjacent surfaces of two members or components, typically joined and held together by nails, glue, screws, or mortar.

Joist. One of a series of parallel beams, usually 2 inches thick and placed on the edge to support the floor in selling loads and supported, in turn, by large beams, girders, or bearing walls.

Kerf. The slot; a saw's kerf is the thickness of its blade; a drip kerf is cut into the underside of a sill to cause the water to drain free.

Laminating. Applying a plastic laminate to the core material. In framing, nailing two or more pieces of lumber together to increase the load carrying ability.

Landing. The platform between flights of stairs, or where a flight of stairs ends.

Lath. The building material of wood, metal, gypsum, or insulating board fastened to the frame of a building and serving as a plaster base.

Lattice. A framework of crossed wood pieces or metal strips.

Ledger strip. A strip of lumber nailed along the side of a girder, on which joist ends rest. In construction, the parts of the frame attached to the main house.

Let-in brace. Metal or 1 inch thick board braces notched into studs.

Light. The space in a window sash for the single pane of glass.

Lentel. The horizontal structural member that supports the load over an opening such as a door or window. Also called a "header."

Lookout. A short, wood bracket or cantilever that supports the overhanging portion of a roof or similar structure; usually concealed from view.

Louver. An opening with a series of horizontal slats pitched to permit ventilation but exclude rain, sunlight, or vision.

Lumber, dressed size. The dimensions of lumber after it is shrunk from its green dimensions and after machining to size of a pattern.

Lumber, matched. Lumber dressed and shaped on one edge into a groove pattern and in tongued pattern on the other.

Lumber, shiplap. Lumber edge-dressed to make a close, rabbeted or lapped joint.

Lumber, timber yard. Lumber 5 inches or more in the shortest to dimension. The term may include beams, stringers, post, sills, girders, and purlins.

Lumber, yard. Lumber of a grade, size, and pattern usually intended for ordinary construction, for example, framework and rough coverage of houses.

Mantel. The shelf above the fireplace.

Margin. To center a window or door frame in the thickness of the wall so that frame edges are flush with finish surfaces on both sides, or so frame edges protrude equally.

Masonry. Stone, brick concrete, hollow tile, concrete block, gypsum block, or a combination of these materials bonded together with mortar to form a wall, pier, buttress, or simular mass.

Mastic. A pasty material used as a cement (as for setting tile) or a protective coating (as for thermal insulation or waterproofing).

Migration. The movement of a jack, or structural member due to the loads upon it; a dangerous situation if the jack is not plumb.

Millwork. Generally, any building material made of finished wood and manufactured in millwork plants and planning mills; the term covers such items as doors, windows and door-frames, blinds, porchwork, mantels, paneling, stairways, molding, and trim, but normally not flooring or siding.

Miter joint. The joint of two pieces set in an angle that bisects the joining angle. For example, butt 90° miter joint of the side in head casing at a door opening is made up of two 45° angles.

Molding. A shaped wood strip used for decoration.

Mortise. A slot cut in a board, plank, or timber, usually edgewise, to receive the tenon of another board, plank, or timber.

Mullion. A vertical bar or divider in the frame between windows, doors, or other openings.

Muntin. A small member that divides the glass over openings, sashes or doors.

Newel. This small port to which the end of a stair railing or balustrade is fastened.

Non-bearing wall. A wall supporting no other than its own weight.

Nosing. Usually, the project an image of a stair tread.

On-center (OC). The measurement of spacing for studs, rafters, joists, and so on in building, from the center of one member to the center of the next.

Outrigger. The extension of a rafter beyond the wall line; usually a smaller rafter nailed to a larger one, forming a cornice or roof overhang.

Paint. A combination of pigments with suitable thinners or oils; used as a decorative and protective coating.

Paper, building. A general term indicating such sheet materials as rosin papers and felts.

Parting stop are stripped. The small wood pieces in the jambs of double-hung window frames to separate upper and lower sashes.

Partition. A wall that subdivide spaces within any story of a house.

Penny. As applied to nails, originally indicating the price per hundred; term is now a measurement and is abbreviated "d."

Pier. A column of masonry used to support other structural members.

Pitch. The inclined slope of a roof, or the ratio of the total rise to the total width of a house.

Plaster grounds. Strips of wood used as guides or strike off edges around window and door openings and around the base of walls.

Plate. Sill plate; a horizontal member anchored to the masonary wall. So plates or shoe; the lowest horizontal member of the framed wall. Top plate; the highest horizontal member of the framed wall, which supports ceiling joists, rafters, or other members.

Plough. To cut a length-wise groove in a board or a plank.

Plumb. Exactly perpendicular; vertical.

Preservative. Any substance that prevents the action of wood-destroying fungi or insects.

Primer. The base coat of paint in the paint job; consist of two or more coats.

Quarter-round. A small molding that has the cross section of a ¼-circle.

Rabbet. A rectangular, longitudinal groove cut in the edge of a board plank.

Radiant heating. A method of heating, usually consisting of a force hot water system with pipes placed in the floor, wall, or ceiling; or with electrically heated panels.

Rafter. One of the series of structural members of a roof designed to support roof loads. The rafters of a flat roof are sometimes called a roof joist.

Rafter, hip. A rafter that forms the intersection of an external roof angle.

Rafter, valley. A rafter that forms the intersection of an internal roof angle. Valley rafters are usually doubled 2 inch thick members.

Rail. Horizontal framing members of a panel door, sash, or a cabinet frame. Also the upper and lower members of an oval balustrade or staircase extending from one vertical support (such as a post) to another.

Rake. Trim members that run parallel to roof slope and form the finish between the wall and a gable-roof extension.

Reinforcement. Steel rods or fabric of metal placed in concrete slabs, beams, or columns to increase their strength.

Ridge. Horizontal line at the junction of the top edges of two sloping roof surfaces.

Ridge board. The board placed on edge at the ridge of the roof, to which the upper ends of rafters are fastened.

Rise. In stairs, the vertical height of a step or flight of stairs.

Riser. Each of several vertical boards used to close the space between stairway treads.

Roll roofing. Roofing material composed of asphalt saturated fiber supplied in 36 inch wide rolls, with 108 square feet of material.

Roof sheathing. Boards or sheet material fastened to the roof rafters on wood shingles or other roof coverings are laid.

Rough opening (RO). A framed opening in a wall, roof, or a platform.

Run. In stairs, the net width of a step or the horizontal distance covered by a flight of stairs.

Sash. A frame containing one or more panes of glass.

Sash balance. A device, usually operated by a spring or weight, designed to counterbalance the weight of a window sash.

Saturated felt. A felt impregnated with tar or asphalt.

Screed. A small strip of wood, usually the thickness of a plaster coat, use as a guide for plastering. Also a board used to level newly laid concrete.

Scribing. Fitting woodwork to an irregular surface.

Sealer. A finishing material, clear or pigmented, usually applied directly over uncoated wood to seal the surface.

Semigloss paint or enamel. Paint or enamel that has some luster but which isn't particularly glossy.

Shake. Thick handsplit shingle.

Shear wall. A wall reinforced to withstand lateral (shear) movement such as that felt during an earthquake.

Sheathing. Structural covering, usually wood boards or plywood, used over studs, joists or rafters of a structure.

Sheet metal work. All components of a house made of sheet metal, for example, flashing, gutters, and downspouts.

Shoe. Base molding used next to the floor on the interior base board. Also the bottom plate of the framed wall.

Shy. To cut something a bit short.

Siding. The finished covering of the outside wall of a frame building, whether made of clapboards, vertical boards with battens, shingles, or some other material.

Sill. In framing (also called the "mudsill"), the lowest member of a frame of a structure; it rests on the foundation and supports the floor joists or the uprights of the wall. In door or window construction, the member, forming and the lowest side of the opening, as the window sill or doorsill.

Sleeper. Usually, the wood member embedded in or placed on concrete, to which the subflooring or floorinng is attached.

Soffit. Usually the underside of an overhang cornice.

Soil cover. Also called "ground cover," the light covering of plastic film, roll roofing, or similar material used over the soil in crawl spaces of houses to minimize moisture permeation of the area.

Span. The distance between structural supports, such as walls, columns, piers, beams, girders, and trusses.

Splash blocking. A small masonary block placed beneath a downspout, carrying water away from the building.

Square. A unit of measurement (100 square feet) usually applied to roofing material in measurement to adjacent pieces that join at a right angle.

Stair carriage. Supporting member for stair treads. Usually the 2-inch thick plank notched to receive the treads.

Stile. An upright framing member in the panel door, sash, or a cabinet frame.

Stock. The basic materials from which a building element is fashioned. For example, joist may be cut from 2 x 4 stock, or flashing may be cut from 26 gauge aluminum stock.

Stool. The flat molding, usually rabbeted on the underside, that fits over the inside edge of a window sill.

Storm sash or storm window. An extra window usually placed on the outside of an existing one as additional protection against cold air.

Strip flooring. Wood covering consisting of narrow, matched strips.

Stringer. In stairs, the supports in which stairs ends rest, more or less synonymous with "carriage."

Strong. To cut something a bit long.

Stucco. A plaster made of Portland cement as its base; used outside.

Stud. One of the series of slender, wood or metal, vertical structural members placed as supporting elements in walls and partitions.

Subfloor. Boards or plywood laid over joists, over which the finish is laid.

Suspended ceiling. The ceiling system supported by being hung from overhead structural framing.

Termite shield. A shield, usually of corrosion resistant metal, placed in or on a foundation wall or other mass of masonary or around pipes, to prevent termite migration.

Ternplate. Sheet iron or steel coated with an alloy of lead and tin.

Threshold. A strip of wood or metal with beveled edges, usually over the finish floor and sill of exterior doors.

Toe nailing. To drive any nail in at an angle, thereby preventing it from pulling free.

Tread. A horizontal board in a stairway, on which one steps.

Trim. The finish material in the building, such as molding applied around openings, window trim, door trim, baseboards, and cornices.

Trimmer. Any structural member added to decrease flexion along the length of rough openings. In floor framing, the outermost joist running parallel to the joist grid.

Truss. A frame or jointed structure of smaller elements designed to span long distances.

Undercoat. A coating applied before the finish or top coat of paint.

Underlayment. A material placed under finnish coverings, expecially thin floor materials, to provide a smooth, even base.

Valley. The internal angle formed by the junction of two sloping sides of a roof.

Vapor barrier. Material used to retard the movement of water vapor into walls and thus prevent condensation in them.

Printed in the United States
By Bookmasters